Low Glycemic Happiness

Low Glycemic Happiness

120 Custom-Crafted Low Glycemic Load Recipes for Health and Happiness

By
Dr. Maury Breecher
and
Judy Lickus, BS

Published by
Diabetes Manager, LLC
Corpus Christi, TX 78412

Notice

Diabetes Manager, LLC has published this book to provide information regarding the subject matter covered. It is sold with the understanding that the publisher and the authors are not liable for the misconception or misuse of any information provided. Every effort has been made to make this book as complete and as accurate as possible. The purpose of this book is to educate. The authors of *Low Glycemic Happiness* and its' publisher *Diabetes Manager, LLC* shall have neither liability nor responsibility to any person or entity with respect to any loss, damage, or injury caused or alleged to be caused directly or indirectly by the information contained in this book. The information presented here is in no way intended as a substitute for medical treatment or nutritional counseling.

The mention of specific companies, organizations, or authorities in this book does not imply endorsement by the authors or publisher, nor does mention of specific companies, organizations, or authorities imply their endorsement of this book.

Internet addresses and directions cited in this book were accurate at the time this book went to press.

ISBN: 0615731899
ISBN-13: 9780615731896
Library of Congress Control Number: 2012955437

Published in Corpus Christi and Dallas, Texas
by *Diabetes Manager, LLC*.

Cover, back cover, page design and production by *CreateSpace*

DEDICATION

We dedicate this book to Tom Stutzman, who was one of the first to try our authentic original *Low Glycemic Load* recipes.

It was a joy to watch his progress!

For a year, he consistently demonstrated that he understood the principles of our Low GL program. He prepared the recipes using the ingredients and preparation instructions we provided.

The result was fantastic as we watched his excess weight melt away. He not only lost the 75 pounds he wanted to drop off, his health improved, too. His medical doctor ordered laboratory tests which revealed that Tom's blood chemistries had improved dramatically, going from red to green among most measures in just a few short months.

His success, and his technical help with computer and video issues, enabled and inspired us as we completed *Low Glycemic Happiness*.

PREFACE

Author's Story:
High *Glycemic Load* (GL) Eating Led to this Book

I (Breecher) draw on two sides of myself: My personal life as an individual with type 2 diabetes and my professional experience as a medical/health reporter, editor, and co-author of 11 published books including Dr. James W. Anderson's *Live Longer Better* and Dr. Alan Lazar's, *Beyond the Knife: Alternatives to Surgery.*

For almost two decades as a person with type 2 diabetes I have lived with sugar highs and lows, and have experienced the frustration and stress involved in trying to maintain healthy blood sugar levels throughout the day, every day and every night.

Since my diagnosis of type 2 diabetes in 1995, I followed *the American Diabetes Association*'s recommended Food Exchange Diet, the *American Heart Association's* low fat diet, and other diets and food plans recommended by experts and medical authorities. Yet, despite occasional short-term weight loss, overall I steadily accumulated excess weight.

How did I – and the majority of us North Americans (60%), get so fat?

The common denominator in all the eating programs mentioned above is that all recommend low fat, high carbohydrate eating plans. In spite, or maybe because of those eating programs, I gained excess weight year after year and experienced stressful sugar highs and lows that continually battered my body.

Of course, I and most of the rest of the overweight people in North America had been following the same conventional wisdom from respected health institutions given for 30 years to all Americans – eat a low fat, high carbohydrate diet with 60% of our daily calorie intake from carbohydrate.

There was logic behind those recommendations. Since cardiovascular diseases kill most people and CVD seemed to be caused by high intakes of dietary fat, the recommendations made sense for many years.

However, they don't make sense now. The results have been disastrous. For instance, Will Lassek, MD, a former Assistant Surgeon General, writing in a 2012 *Psychology Today*, says that Americans were 25 pounds heavier in 2012 than they were in the mid-1970's.

Marion Nestle, PhD, chairperson of the Nutrition Department of New York University and author of *How the Food Industry Influences Nutrition and Health*, blames the failure of nutrition authorities to educate Americans about the health differences between *saturated* fats and *unsaturated* fats.

"The idea was to reduce saturated fat, but the assumption was that it was too complicated to explain all that [to the public], and that if people just reduced the fat content of their diet, they would be improving it," she told *Frontline*.

What the experts didn't expect, continued Dr. Nestle in her *Frontline* appearance, was that the food industry would substitute vegetable fats for animal fats and substitute carbohydrates such as sugar for fats, while keeping the calorie content of the products "exactly the same."

Americans are now ingesting less fat while eating more carbohydrate-based foods, according to the US Department of Agriculture *(USDA)*. According to the 2012 report, Americans are eating 10g less fat per day today than they were [eating] in the late 1970's. The percentage of total calories derived from fat declined substantially from 39.7% to 33.4% between 1977 and 2008.

So what is making us fat? My vote goes to the sweet tooth that all humans have, especially we in North America. According to the New Hampshire Department of Health and Human Services, two hundred years ago the average American ate only two pounds of sugar a year. In 1970, we ate 123 pounds of sugar per year. Today, the average American consumes almost 152 pounds of sugar a year. This is equal to three pounds (or six cups) of sugar consumed in one week!

Those figures don't even consider the impact of all the white flour, potatoes, pasta, bread and other high glycemic foods which our bodies' convert into sugar! At one time I was right alongside most other Americans shoveling sugar or those other high glycemic foods into my ever expanding stomach.

I wish I had known about low glycemic eating back then. Apparently, years before my actual diagnosis of type 2 diabetes, I suffered the stresses of blood sugar highs and lows for years long before the diagnosis of diabetes in 1995. Attempting to maintain healthy blood sugar levels during those years without knowing the best foods and correct portion sizes to eat for steady blood sugar levels resulted in constant stressors that played havoc with my body, mind, and emotions, interfering with my ability to feel happy.

When I ate the wrong foods, or even too much of the right ones, my energy dwindled and my emotions, especially my patience levels, became harder for me to handle, wrecking my feelings of happiness and, often, the happiness of others with whom I came into contact. This was especially true regarding the four patient and loving women I married and was divorced from during the years in which I was pre-diabetic and then diabetic. The disease – with its' mood altering ups and downs –often made it difficult for me to appreciate, let alone return their love and patience.

If your doctor has told you that you are *pre-diabetic* (at the tipping point between good health and full-blown diabetes), you don't have to follow in my footsteps. Type 2 diabetes doesn't occur overnight. It silently develops over years of overindulgent eating and lack of exercise. You can learn from my mistakes.

Proper eating of *low glycemic load* foods in appropriate portions in combination with regular exercise can save you from this disease. Or, if you already have diabetes, eating a diet predominantly composed of *low glycemic load (LGL) meals* can help you control your blood sugar levels to the point where you may be able to, with your physician's guidance, lower your own need for insulin or diabetic oral medications. I have. With my doctor's knowledge, by eating *LGL meals* on a daily basis, I reduced the amount of insulin I take and have weaned myself from dependence on several widely prescribed oral diabetic medications.

Grab this chance to eat the *authentic Low Glycemic Load (LGL) way*. Don't let diabetes over years of time creep up on you as it did to me.

The years between 1995 to the present have been rife with academic and professional arguments between various experts and authorities on the pros and cons of *low glycemic* and *high glycemic* as well as low and high carbohydrate diets and when each should be used. I have come to the personal conclusion that most of the health benefits of low carbohydrate diets actually occur because low carb meals are *low glycemic load*.

In my opinion, in light of the June 2013 agreements by a recent Consensus panel of international medical and nutritional experts and evidence from many studies by multiple medical institutions, those arguments should end. LGL recipes should be recommended to all patients who could benefit from them. You'll learn more about that Consensus panel's conclusions in the Introduction.

In Appendix B, you can, if you want to, learn more about research into the science and value of low glycemic eating and how it can enhance your health and happiness. We also tell you a bit about the development of the *Glycemic Index* and the later refinement of the idea by Harvard experts who developed the concept of *glycemic load*.

So, read and enjoy as much or as little of the narrative sections of *Low Glycemic Happiness* as you want. More importantly look at, choose, cook, and enjoy our easy-to-prepare, tasty recipes. You will be glad you did.

Maury M. Breecher, PhD, MPH

ACKNOWLEDGEMENTS

The authors extend our profound thanks and appreciation to the following individuals (in alphabetical order) who contributed significantly to our project in many ways:

- Pam Arredondo
- Chris Breecher
- Martin Breecher
- Michael Breecher
- Susan Burkett
- Erica Butron
- Ruth Courtis
- Annette Elton
- Don Flint
- Matthew Hagar
- Sherry Howe
- Grady Hunter
- Stephanie Korney
- Kay Leushner
- Melissa Lickus
- Judi Wilder
- Ernest Lowe
- Jennifer Record
- Katie Silcox
- Tom Stutzman
- Donna Suthard
- Cindy Welch
- Carroll Wilkerson
- Karen Wilson

Of all the ingredients our recipe creators studied, researched, and tasted in the development of these recipes, the most important is the love they added.

Maury M Breecher, PhD, MPH and Judith M Lickus, BS, LBSW

INTRODUCTION

What If We All Changed Our Eating Habits for Better Health and Happiness?

Would that Make Our Lives *"Just Right"*?

Leading medical and nutrition experts from around the world, meeting in Italy in June 2013, for the first time in history reached a consensus agreeing that Low Glycemic Load (LGL) eating decreases your risks of obesity, heart disease, and diabetes.

Furthermore, the experts agreed that if you have already developed type 2 diabetes, LGL eating can help you better manage that disease, obesity, and cardiovascular disease.

If you changed your eating habits for the better, wouldn't you be taking a giant step to making your life "just right," happier and healthier?

The Consensus experts are in the forefront of a new wave of understanding about the glycemic impact of carbohydrates in the human bloodstream and its health consequences. That wave of understanding may revolutionize our food choices, the dietary advice provided by the American Diabetes and the American Heart Associations, and even the nutritional information distributed by U.S. governmental agencies and institutes.

When *You* act on that new understanding based on knowledge available in this book, *you* will be exercising your God-given guaranteed right to pursue happiness. You will be rewarded with a tool that can be used to reduce the risks of developing Obesity, Coronary Heart Disease (CHD), and Type 2 diabetes, or, if you already have CHD and Type 2 diabetes, you will be better able to manage those conditions.

A giant step toward making those promises a reality for the millions of individuals who have those disorders occurred when, after two days of discussion and final agreements the panel of international experts issued a *Consensus Statement* proclaiming:

> "The *Glycemic Load (GL)* is the single best
> predictor of the glycemic response of foods."

The International Glycemic Panel is composed of scientists writing for other scientists. I write mostly for consumers. Here in plain talk is my interpretation of the statement above:

> The Glycemic Load (GL) is the single best predictor of the [human body's] *response* [*to the glucose contained in carbohydrate-based food*].

O.K., so now we know the scientists are referring to foods that are carbohydrate-based. That means they are talking about foods from growing things ranging from grains to fruits and vegetables.

By *glycemic response,* the scientists are referring to what happens when the human body converts carbohydrate-based foods including those made from grains – such as bread, cereal, pasta, pizza and pastries – as well as carbohydrate foods known collectively as *fruits and vegetables.*

When humans eat carbohydrate, the digestion process releases glucose, often called *blood sugar* because it is released into the bloodstream.

The *glycemic response* is the *how high* and *how fast* blood sugar levels increase depending on the source of the carbohydrate (fruit, vegetables, grains, baked goods, sugared soda) and *how much* is ingested – that's the *Glycemic Load.* Wow, that's very important knowledge if you have diabetes . . . or even if you don't.

Why This Is Important

Why? Two major medical disorders have reached epidemic proportions throughout the world – obesity and type 2 diabetes. Both can, and often do, lead to coronary heart and artery disease, heart attacks and strokes.

What those diseases have in common is that high blood sugar levels over time can lead to obesity, coronary heart disease, diabetes, and a number of other nasty related disorders called comorbidities.

The amazing thing is that your risks for developing those diseases are greatly reduced when you mostly eat *low glycemic load* meals, instead of high glycemic load meals.

For the first time in history leading scientists have agreed–(at the international panel of experts at the Consensus Meeting in Italy) that eating low GI/ GL foods can:

- Help people lose excess weight
- Reduce the risks of type 2 diabetes, cardiovascular disease, and heart attacks
- Improve glycemic control in those who already have type 2 diabetes. (In other words, if you already have type 2 diabetes, under your doctor's supervision you may be able to reduce your diabetes medications).

So, How Does One Identify Low Glycemic Load Foods?

It turns out that after 33 years of research most carbohydrate foods have been tested, identified and listed in the *Glycemic Index*. However, because the importance of the *Glycemic Load factor* wasn't recognized until recently, most "Low Glycemic" cookbooks are filled with recipes that include too much carbohydrate to really be *Low Glycemic Load meals*. (Apparently the writers of those cookbooks didn't realize that even low glycemic foods can raise blood sugar levels and cause weight gain when eaten without regard to an acceptable low glycemic load serving size.)

Why did such a simple fact take so long to be understood by the experts?

Well, there was the "missing ingredient," the *how to figure* the *Glycemic Load* calculation.

It has taken almost two decades for scientists to reach agreement about this "missing ingredient". That's why the Consensus Statement proclaimed by the International Panel of Glycemic experts is such a big step forward.

The new system was developed by a team of researchers led by world famous researcher Walter Willett, MD, a professor and chair of Epidemiology at Harvard University School of Public Health. The Harvard researchers realized that a method was needed to quantify the amount at which a low glycemic food starts having medium or even high glycemic effects.

They named that variable the *Glycemic Load*. The GL reveals whether certain amounts of specific carbohydrate are low glycemic or not. For instance, a small red apple is low glycemic, but eating a large one will spike one's blood sugar. It not low glycemic load.

To determine the *Glycemic Load* of a meal, one has to look up the *Glycemic Index* (GI) rankings of the foods in the meal and determine the amount of carbohydrate contained in the meal. Then, a calculation using those elements determines the *Glycemic Load* (GL).

The result is 100 times more accurate in predicting *glycemic response*. It is such a powerful predictor that once you know how to use it, it allows you to monitor what you eat and easily predict its effect on your blood glucose levels. We explain how to do that in Appendix A.

This Is of Vital Importance to People with Diabetes or Pre-Diabetes

The Consensus experts stated that "The carbohydrate quality as defined by GI/GL is particularly important for individuals who are sedentary, overweight and at increased risk of diabetes."

High glycemic foods "spike" blood sugar levels….but high blood sugar levels can also result if one eats too much of even low glycemic foods. That's why knowing the *glycemic load* can be of benefit to people with diabetes.

The Consensus experts stated that:

> "There is *convincing evidence*" from a large body of research "that Low GI/GL diets:
> - Help control blood glucose levels in people with diabetes,
> - Reduces risk of developing type 2 diabetes and
> - Reduces risk of coronary heart disease (improves blood lipids and inflammation) and
> - May also help with "body weight management."

Scientists believe that the most likely mechanism for how LGL diets may reduce type 2 diabetes is that "low GI/GL diets improve insulin sensitivity and beta-cell function (the cells on the pancreas which manufacture insulin) in people who have type 2 diabetes and in those who have *pre-diabetes*.

For you folks who have diabetes or have been told that you are *pre-diabetic*, it is vitally important to be able to predict how high carbohydrate foods will raise your blood sugar levels. You want to take steps to limit high blood sugar levels.

That's why the Glycemic Load is the foundation for all of the recipes in this book. We present 120 custom-crafted low GL recipes and 30 snacks and provide both the GI and GL scores of each recipe. Using these recipes and developing your own using the guidelines in Appendix A could help you stay off of insulin if your body doesn't yet need insulin injections. On the other hand, if your physician has already prescribed external insulin, changing your diet by predominantly eating LGL meals may help reduce your need for external insulin and perhaps eliminate it over time.

A Metaphor on the Benefits by Eating *Low GL Happiness* Foods

To "see" the difference between the *impact* of *low*, compared to *high glycemic load* foods, think of your body as a locomotive; carbohydrates are the fuel. Think of carbohydrates as the chunks of wood and coal that burn to keep the locomotive moving.

In order to run your engine – that is, your body and brain – efficiently, you want to use a fuel that burns very slowly so it will last a long time. *Low Glycemic Load* (LGL) foods are like slow-burning wood. As your body uses low GL foods, it releases glucose very slowly. With low GL foods, your body burns glucose at a nice slow rate and runs smoothly, over an extended period of time.

In contrast, eating *high glycemic load* foods is like pouring gasoline-soaked coal on a fire. The "fire" burns very hot, but dies down quickly. Here's what occurs: In your body, HGL foods trigger spikes in your blood glucose levels. Glucose is the fuel that powers your body. The hormone known as insulin is like gasoline since it is the catalyst that starts the "burn" or metabolism of glucose in your body. It does that by transporting glucose through the bloodstream into cells where it is burned to provide energy for cellular processes. Excess glucose is converted into glycogen for storage in the liver or converted into fat.

Resulting plunges in blood glucose levels make many people susceptible to fatigue and depression. To relieve those feelings, they may eat high-sugar snacks or other HGL foods. Those high glucose foods again spike blood sugar levels to higher than healthy levels. That triggers the pancreas to produce more insulin. Those high to low and back again swings in blood glucose can, over years of time, exhaust the insulin-producing cells of the pancreas AND influence the cells of muscles and other body tissues to become *resistant* to insulin.

When elevated levels of glucose remain in the blood, that condition of high blood sugar is known as *hyperglycemia*. *Hyperglycemia* triggers the beta cells of the pancreas to produce more insulin. Over time *insulin resistance* and *hyperglycemia* can lead to type 2 diabetes and Metabolic Syndrome, a condition characterized by an excess of abdominal fat, high blood pressure, high levels of cholesterol and triglycerides, and low levels of the good cholesterol known as high density lipoprotein (HDL). The end result of uncontrolled blood glucose swings can be increased risks for heart and artery diseases and for diabetes and its serious complications including blindness, kidney disease, and painful and infected limbs.

Although *Low Glycemic Happiness* recipes are suitable for almost everyone who can safely enjoy low levels of carbohydrate, when we developed these recipes particularly on our minds were the:

- 25.8 million Americans who, like Dr. Breecher, have Type 2 diabetes, according to the American Diabetes Association (ADA)

- 79 million Americans who, according to the *ADA*, are *pre-diabetic* – on the tipping point of developing full-blown diabetes

- 314 million people worldwide who, according to the World Health Organization (WHO), have pre-diabetes

- 347 million people worldwide, according to WHO, who have passed the tipping point and have developed diabetes.

Are you in one of the above groups?

Have a Side Order of Happiness

Low *GL* foods not only keep you strong and bright, they *decrease* the risks of developing subclinical depression and also protect against Depression, a serious disease of the emotions.

For instance, scientists at the Jean Mayer USDA Human Nutrition Research Center on Aging at Tufts University, Boston, were interested in comparing the effects of *high glycemic (HG)* and *low glycemic (LG)* dieting on people. They devised a six-month randomized controlled trial in which all the food was provided to 42 subjects (all healthy but overweight males from ages 30 to 40) whom were being studied. The researchers assessed mood states by using the Profile of Mood States (POMS) questionnaire. The researchers found "Worsening mood outcome over time ... in the (HG) diet group compared to the LG group for the Depression subscale. . ."

The researchers continued saying:

"These findings suggest a negative effect of a HG weight-loss diet on sub-clinical depression."

The opposite of HG eating is *low glycemic* eating. *Low glycemic load* eating is the way nature intended us to eat. Adopting a low *GL* lifestyle allows you to eliminate or greatly reduce the emotional ups and downs caused by fluctuating blood sugars. As a result, you enjoy *increased* energy and stamina, and may even discover that you are thinking better, making better decisions and, as a result, are happier. This side order of happiness is just a sweet side effect.

As Goldilocks said . . ."it was *just right.*"

Introducing Our *Low Glycemic Happiness Recipe Collection*

Here's What Is in This Wonderful Book

Our *Low Glycemic Happiness Recipe Collection* contains a custom-crafted set of 120 low GL recipes and an additional batch of 30+ (mostly grab-and-go) low GL snacks. Each recipe is introduced by its' *bold-faced* GI ranking (always at 55 or under) and its' *bold-faced* GL score (always at 10 or less), and each recipe delivers 30g of carbs or less. Those numbers represent your assurance that the recipes in this book are genuinely low GL.

Right under the bold-faced *Glycemic Index* ranking and *Glycemic Load* score, you will see the rest of each recipe's nutrient data per serving including calorie counts, grams of carbohydrate, fiber, saturated fat, protein and milligrams of sodium.

Following the *Low Glycemic Happiness Recipe Collection*, you will find, in Appendix A, a detailed blueprint of how you can build your own Low GL Roast Turkey Dinner. By following the steps you will also be teaching yourself how to build your own Low GL recipes.

Appendix B provides even more information on some of the many vital *health and happiness* enhancing benefits that the *just right eating* of *low glycemic load* menus can bring into *your* life.

Appendix C provides a brief history of Glycemic research.

Appendix D informs you that the recipes in this book are the *lowest of the low in terms of both glycemic impact and carbohydrate count*. For that reason, you are warned, that if you use this book to lose excess weight, to eat at least 130 mg of carbohydrate per day, a task easy to do if you don't skip meals, eat low glycemic load side dishes with lunch and/or dinner, and partake of the recommended snacks that are listed.

The creation of the recipes in *Low Glycemic Happiness* took into consideration the latest information on the roles played by the *Glycemic Index* (GI) and the *Glycemic Load* (GL). That information allowed us to choose healthy low *GL* foods that enhance your health by fueling your body with the *just right amount* (*the load*) of carbohydrate that your body needs to convert blood sugar into energy within the cells of your body. Choosing not only the *just right* foods, but also the *just right amounts* (the *glycemic loads*) of those foods is important. Doing so supports your highest levels of health and happiness.

There are many roads to happiness, but one thing is certain: When you travel the road to increased happiness it makes the trip easier to recognize that happiness is in the journey – the *just right*, easy, enjoyable, and fun cooking journey – as well as at your destination, a tasty meal and a satisfied appetite.

Enjoy your trip through these health and happiness-enhancing low GL recipes.

CONTENTS

CONTENTS

WAKE UP
TO YOUR DAY

BREAKFAST

ASPARAGUS OMELET

YIELD: Serves 1

Per portion:

GI: 40
GL: 2.4

CALORIES: 378; Carbohydrates: 6g; Fiber: 2g; Protein: 15g; Fat: 33.5g; Saturated Fat: 13.5; Sodium: 90mg

INGREDIENTS:

- 8 stalks fresh asparagus
- 2 large eggs, whisked – select organic when available
- 1 tbsp. ground flaxseed
- 4 tbsp. water
- 1 tbsp. extra virgin olive oil
- 1 tbsp. unsalted organic butter

PREPARATION:

1. In a small colander, rinse and drain asparagus; break into bite size pieces; discard woody stalks.
2. Pour olive oil into small stainless steel skillet, coating cooking surface.
3. Add flaxseeds and sauté over medium heat for a few seconds. Pour in water.
4. Place asparagus pieces in pan. Cover and steam for 1 minute, adding more water if necessary.
5. Melt butter in skillet. Pour whisked egg into skillet, cover. Reduce heat to low and cook until edges are set and bubbly.
6. Turn heat off, place cover tightly on pan and allow to rest over warm burner until entire omelet is set.

YOGURT MUSHROOM SOUFFLE'

YIELD: Serves 2

Per portion:

GI: 40
GL: 3.25

CALORIES: 344; Carbohydrates: 8.13g; Fiber: 1g; Protein: 17.5g; Fat: 26g; Saturated Fats: 10.5g; Sodium: 234mg

INGREDIENTS:

- 4 oz. The Greek Gods® Greek Yogurt Traditional Plain (in the green container)
- 1/2 cup chopped fresh mushrooms
- 2 oz. red onion, chopped
- 1 oz. cheddar cheese, grated
- 3 fresh extra-large eggs
- 1 ½ tbsp. water
- 1 tbsp. extra virgin olive oil
- 1/2 tsp. freshly ground black peppercorns, to taste

PREPARATION:

1. Coat a medium skillet with olive oil. Preheat skillet over low heat.
2. Add onion and mushrooms, sauté over low heat for 1 minute.
3. Remove onion and mushrooms to a small bowl.
4. In another small bowl, whisk the eggs, yogurt, water and freshly ground black peppercorns until fluffy.
5. Add the egg mixture to the preheated skillet in a circular motion. Cover.
6. As the eggs begin to set, allow the liquid part to run underneath from time to time, while gently pulling the top edges away from the sides as you tilt the pan.

7. When the omelet is set, add the prepared filling down the center. Sprinkle with cheese.
8. Cover the pan and let omelet rest for a few minutes over very low heat until the cheese melts.
9. Lift the skillet's handle slightly, and with a spatula, assist the omelet so that it folds itself in half. Turn off the heat.
10. Divide omelet equally onto 2 serving plates. Serve immediately.

CRAB CAKE MONTEREY

YIELD: Serves 2

Per portion:

GI: 40
GL: 2

CALORIES: 497; Carbohydrates: 5g; Fiber: 1.5g; Protein: 40g; Fat: 33
Saturated Fats: 11g; Sodium: 610mg

INGREDIENTS:

- 6.5 oz. can crabmeat, drained
- 3 oz. shredded low-fat Monterey Jack cheese
- 2 tbsp. finely chopped onion
- 2 tbsp. finely chopped celery
- 2 tbsp. finely chopped red bell pepper
- 1 cup egg substitute
- 1/2 tsp. ground paprika
- 2 sprig of fresh parsley, chopped very fine
- 2 tbsp. extra virgin olive oil
- 2 tbsp. Land O'Lakes® Light Butter with Canola Oil

PREPARATION:

1. Coat cooking surface of skillet with olive oil, and preheat over medium heat.
2. Add onion, celery, parsley and red bell pepper to preheated skillet. Cover, and cook over medium heat for a minute until vegetables become crisp-tender.
3. Remove vegetables to a small bowl and cover to keep warm.
4. Add the crabmeat and butter to the skillet, and heat uncovered for 2 minutes, until portions of crabmeat begin to brown.
5. Transfer the crabmeat to a small bowl, and cover to keep warm.
6. Add the egg substitute to the skillet, and reduce heat to medium low. Cover and cook for about 3 minutes.

7. With a spatula, lift the edges of the omelet, and allow any uncooked egg to flow below the cooked portion, while you tilt the skillet. Cover, and continue to cook over low heat until eggs are thoroughly cooked.
8. Arrange the crabmeat and vegetables on top of half of the omelet, and sprinkle the cheese on top. Allow omelet to rest over very low heat for a minute or two until the cheese melts.
9. Fold the plain half of the omelet over the half with the filling.
10. Divide the omelet evenly into two halves and place on 2 serving plates.

DYLAN'S CHEESE AND TOMATO DELIGHT

YIELD: Serves 2

Per portion:

GI: 51
GL: 9.52

CALORIES: 379; Carbohydrates: 18.66g; Fiber: 10g; Protein: 18.5g; Fat: 27g; Saturated Fats: 8.5g; Sodium: 407mg

INGREDIENTS:

- 2 oz. fresh avocado slices
- 2 oz. fresh tomato, in two thin slices
- 1 oz. cheddar cheese, shredded
- 2 extra-large eggs
- 2 slices 100% Whole Grain Bread (produced by Natural Ovens®, USA), toasted
- 2 tbsp. Land'O Lakes® Spreadable Butter with Olive Oil
- 2 sprigs fresh sweet basil for garnish
- 1 tbsp. extra virgin olive oil
- 1/8 tsp. freshly ground black peppercorns, to taste
- 1 clove peeled fresh garlic

PREPARATION:

1. Preheat broiler. Toast bread; rub garlic clove briskly over each slice of toast leaving as much garlic residue as possible; spread 1 tbsp. butter on each slice.
2. Arrange slice of tomato on top of toast. Place under broiler for about 2 minutes, until just warmed.
3. Remove tomato and toast from the oven. Sprinkle cheese on top. Add pepper as desired. Place under broiler until cheese bubbles. Turn off the heat and remove each Delight to a serving dish.
4. Cover cooking surface of skillet with olive oil.

5. Preheat skillet over medium-low heat, break eggs into pan, and cook eggs your favorite way.
6. Place one egg on top of each tomato covered, toasted bread slice.
7. Top each serving with 1 oz. fresh avocado slices.
8. Serve immediately.

DELECTABLE BENEDICT OF EGGS

YIELD: Serves 2

Per portion:

GI: 51
GL: 7.29

CALORIES: 396; Carbohydrates: 14.3g; Fiber: 3.4g; Protein: 29.47g; Fat: 23.25; Saturated Fat: 5.5g; Sodium: 765mg

INGREDIENTS:

- 6 slices Jones® Naturally Hickory Smoked Canadian Bacon
- 8 oz. fresh asparagus stalks
- 4 large eggs
- ¼ cup prepared Knorr® Hollandaise Sauce
- 1 slice 100% Whole Grain Bread (produced by Natural Ovens®, USA)
- 1 tbsp. extra virgin olive oil
- Water to cover eggs

PREPARATION:

1. In a small colander, rinse and drain asparagus; discard woody stalks. Steam asparagus in covered steamer basket for 3 to 5 minutes over medium heat, until asparagus is just crisp-tender, or to taste.
2. Coat a three-inch deep skillet with olive oil. Add water to within about one inch of rim. Bring water to a slow boil over medium-high heat.
3. Crack eggs and slowly release egg white and yolk into simmering water. Cover skillet and reduce heat to very low.
4. Prepare Hollandaise Sauce according to package directions.
5. Toast the bread, slice diagonally into two halves, and place each half on a separate serving plate.
6. Warm Canadian bacon in a skillet over low heat for one minute. Place half of Canadian bacon on top of each half of toast.

7. Allow the eggs to poach until they reach your preferred taste (8 minutes total time for firmly cooked). Remove eggs from skillet with a slotted spoon, and place the eggs on top of the Canadian bacon.
8. Arrange asparagus on one side of egg covered Canadian bacon and spoon Hollandaise sauce equally over the tops of the eggs.

HANK'S FAMOUS VEGGIE FRITTATA

YIELD: Serves 2

Per portion:

GI: 50
GL: 9.75

CALORIES: 479.5; Carbohydrates: 19.5g; Fiber: 6.5g; Protein: 24.5g; Fat: 33.5g; Saturated Fats: 11.5g; Sodium: 324mg

INGREDIENTS:

- 3 fresh extra-large eggs, beaten, organic free range preferred
- 1/2 cup avocado, sliced into 4 wedges
- 1/4 cup tomato, sliced into 4 wedges
- 1/4 cup chopped summer squash
- 2 oz. Monterey Jack cheese, shredded,
- 1/4 cup sliced Portobello mushrooms
- 1/4 chopped zucchini
- 1/4 cup frozen baby lima beans, thawed
- 1 tbsp. grated parmesan cheese
- 1 tbsp. chopped onion
- 1 tsp. minced garlic
- 1 tsp. dried oregano leaves, crushed
- 1 tsp. freshly ground black peppercorns, to taste
- 1 tbsp. extra virgin olive oil

PREPARATION:

1. In a small bowl, beat eggs, beans, and cheese until frothy.
2. Place the onions, garlic, and olive oil in a preheated (over medium heat) cast iron skillet, or ovenproof sauté pan. Add the spices. Add the zucchini, squash, and mushrooms, stirring gently to combine. Cover and cook over medium heat, until tender, or to taste, stirring occasionally.

3. Pour the egg, bean and cheese mixture into the skillet, over the vegetables. Tilt the skillet to allow egg mixture to evenly coat bottom of pan.
4. Cover skillet, reduce heat to low, and allow frittata to cook slowly for about 3 minutes.
5. With a spatula, lift edges of frittata to allow uncooked egg mixture to run under cooked portion while tilting skillet. Reduce heat to very low. Continue to cook, covered, until eggs are fully set.
6. Sprinkle on the Jack cheese.
7. Turn oven to Broiler setting.
8. Place the skillet under the broiler. Allow the top of the omelet to brown slightly and the cheese to melt, for about 2 1/2 minutes.
9. Cut frittata in half, and place each half on a serving plate.
10. Serve immediately with half of tomato and avocado wedges on top of each frittata.

HARMONY SMOOTHIE

YIELD: Serves 1

Per portion:

GI: 38
GL: 9.62

CALORIES: 359; Carbohydrates: 25.32g; Fiber: 4.9g; Protein: 33.34g; Fat: 13.86g; Saturated Fats: 1.51g; Sodium: 129mg

INGREDIENTS:

- 8 oz. Silk® Unsweetened Vanilla Soymilk
- 4 ¼ oz. peeled sliced apple
- 1 scoop or packet (1.06 oz.) Harmonized Protein™ by Proventive™ Nutritional Therapies
- 1 tbsp. raw unsalted almond butter
- 2 drops vanilla extract

PREPARATION:

1. Add all ingredients to a blender. Cover.
2. Blend at high speed for one minute, scraping sides as needed, until smooth and thick. Serve immediately.

HONEYBEE'S FAVORITE BREAKFAST

YIELD: Serves 1

Per portion:

GI: 40
GL: 8.8

CALORIES: 536; Carbohydrates: 22g; Fiber: 7g; Protein: 23g; Fat: 40.5g; Saturated Fats: 12g; Sodium: 683mg

INGREDIENTS:

- 2 oz. Jones® All Natural Pork Sausage
- 2 ounce small tomatoes, halved
- 1 slice Healthy Choice® 7 Grain bread
- 1 large egg
- 1/2 tsp. thyme
- 1/2 tsp. sage
- 1/8 tsp. garlic powder
- 1/4 tsp. Mrs. Dash® Southwest Chipotle Seasoning Blend
- 1 tsp. raw hulled sesame seeds
- 1 tbsp. extra virgin olive oil
- olive oil cooking spray
- freshly ground black peppercorns, to taste

PREPARATION:

1. Preheat oven to 350 degrees.
2. Slice tomatoes in half. Spray baking dish for 1/3 second with olive oil cooking spray. Place tomatoes in baking dish, cut sides up.
3. Sprinkle tomatoes with sage, garlic powder, thyme, sesame seeds, seasoning blend and freshly ground black peppercorns.
4. Drizzle olive oil over tomatoes.
5. Add sausages to baking dish. Cover baking dish tightly.

6. Bake for 45 minutes.
7. After baking, lower heat to 200 degrees to keep sausages and tomatoes warm until served.
8. Coat the surface of a small skillet with olive oil. Preheat skillet over medium heat. Add egg and cook to desired consistency.
9. Toast the bread, if desired and serve.

RED WHITE & BLUE BERRY SMOOTH

YIELD: Serves 1

Per portion:

GI: 50
GL: 9.69

CALORIES: 236.5; Carbohydrates: 19.38g; Fiber: 4.6g; Protein: 29.21g; Fat: 8.23g; Saturated Fats: 1.75g; Sodium: 463mg

INGREDIENTS:

- 12 oz. unsweetened coconut milk
- 3 heaping tbsp. MLO Super High Protein Powder
- 3 oz. fresh strawberries, rinsed with leaves removed
- 2 oz. fresh blueberries, rinsed
- 2 oz. silken tofu

PREPARATION:

Place all ingredients in a blender. Cover and blend on high for about a minute, scraping sides as necessary.

DELIGHTFUL QUICHE LORRAINE

YIELD: Serves 6

Per portion:

GI: 40
GL: 5.84

CALORIES: 346.22; Carbohydrates: 14.61g; Fiber: 2.20; Protein: 21.13g; Fat: 26.83g; Saturated Fats: 11.20g; Sodium: 227.5mg

INGREDIENTS:

- 5 slices turkey bacon, cooked and crumbled
- 1 ½ cups nonfat evaporated milk
- 1 ¼ cups shredded low sodium Swiss cheese
- 1 cup Kellogg's All Bran® (manufactured in Battlecreek, MI, USA)
- 1 cup finely chopped yellow onion
- 6 extra-large eggs (about 1 cup), beaten until well combined with a whisk – set aside 2 tbsp. for crust – organic eggs are always preferred
- 4 tbsp. grated Parmesan cheese
- 1 tbsp. apple cider vinegar
- 1 tbsp. almond meal flour
- 2 tbsp. extra virgin olive oil
- 1/2 tsp. ground nutmeg

PREPARATION:

1. Preheat oven to 350 degrees for metal pie pan, or 325 degrees for heat resistant glass pie dish.
2. Spread 1 tbsp. olive oil over cooking surface of the pie dish and place over low medium heat.
3. Add the apple cider vinegar and onion; cover. Cook, stirring occasionally, until onions are tender. Add water if necessary to prevent scorching. Remove pie pan from heat and set aside.

4. Place bran flakes in blender and process on high for a few seconds, until flakes are broken up.
5. Combine 2 tbsp. beaten egg and 2 tbsp. of the Parmesan cheese in a medium sized mixing bowl until well combined. Add bran flake crumbs and almond meal flour; mix thoroughly. You can add a bit more egg to the mixture to form dough for the pie crust.
6. Coat cooking surface of oversized 9 inch pie pan (glass works best) with the second tbsp. olive oil. Pat the dough mixture well over the bottom and a bit up the sides of the pie pan, forming an even layer for the crust. Set aside.
7. In a large mixing bowl, sprinkle the nutmeg over the Swiss cheese and mix well. Add the cooked onions and bacon and mix thoroughly.
8. Thoroughly combine the evaporated milk and beaten eggs separately in a medium sized bowl.
9. Add the evaporated milk and egg mixture to the Swiss cheese mixture and combine well to create the filling.
10. Pour the filling mixture into the crust, and sprinkle with the remaining 2 tbsp. of Parmesan cheese.
11. Bake in oven for about 45 minutes, or until a sharp knife inserted into center comes out clean, and top is golden brown.
12. Divide evenly into 6 servings, and serve on warm serving plates.

FETA MUSHROOM MEDLEY FAVORITE

YIELD: Serves 2

Per portion:

GI: 40
GL: 3.18

CALORIES: 441.25; Carbohydrates: 7.95g; Fiber: 1g; Protein: 21g; Fat: 35g; Saturated Fats: 12g; Sodium: 614.8mg

INGREDIENTS:

- 1 cup mushrooms, rinsed and sliced
- 1/3 cup feta cheese
- 1/4 cup sliced sweet red onion
- 4 extra-large eggs, whisked
- 2 tbsp. extra virgin olive oil
- 1 tbsp. minced garlic
- 1 tsp. curry powder
- 1/8 tsp. of freshly ground black peppercorns, to taste
- 2 sprigs fresh parsley

PREPARATION:

1. Coat cooking surface of skillet with 1 tbsp. olive oil. Preheat skillet over medium heat.
2. Add the onions and garlic to the skillet and sauté for a couple of minutes, stirring occasionally so ingredients do not stick or burn.
3. Add the mushrooms and continue to stir occasionally for about 1 minute.
4. Season mushrooms with the curry powder and freshly ground black peppercorns.
5. Continue to stir to combine flavors for another minute.
6. Remove from burner and pour vegetable mixture onto 2 plates, evenly dividing mushroom medley, covering to keep warm.

7. Coat the cooking surface of the skillet with the 2nd tbsp. of olive oil and preheat over medium-high heat.
8. Add the eggs, reduce heat, and cook the eggs to taste.
9. Sprinkle half of the feta cheese over the eggs.
10. Turn off heat, cover, and allow cheese to melt for about 1 minute.
11. Remove skillet from stove and put 2 eggs on top of each mushroom medley.
12. Sprinkle with remainder of feta cheese.
13. Garnish with fresh parsley sprigs.

VEGETARIAN SAUSAGE SCRAMBLE

YIELD: Serves 1

Per portion:

GI: 40
GL: 4.31

CALORIES: 442; Carbohydrates: 10.79g; Fiber: 7g; Protein: 39g; Fat: 23g; Saturated Fats: 7g; Sodium: 755mg

INGREDIENTS:

- 2 Morningstar Farms® Vegetarian Breakfast Patties
- 1/2 cup diced green bell pepper
- 2 fresh extra-large eggs
- 1 tbsp. Crystal Farms® Spreadable Butter with Canola Oil

PREPARATION:

1. Coat cooking surface of medium sized skillet with butter, and place over medium heat.
2. Add the green pepper and sauté lightly.
3. Using a microwave oven, cook vegetarian breakfast patties according to instructions on package. Remove from microwave and allow cooked patties to cool a bit.
4. In a small bowl, whip eggs until they are well mixed. Add the eggs to the skillet. Cook scrambled eggs until they are firmly set. Reduce heat to very low.
5. Crumble breakfast patties and add to the skillet. Cover tightly for a minute.

SUCCULENT SHELLFISH FLORENTINE

YIELD: Serves 2

Per portion:

GI: 51
GL: 3.57

CALORIES: 362; Carbohydrates: 7; Fiber: 9g; Protein: 31g; Fat: 28.5; Saturated Fat: 3g; Sodium: 181mg

INGREDIENTS:

- 2 cups coarsely chopped fresh spinach
- 6 oz. crabmeat, drained
- 16 stalks fresh asparagus
- 1 cup sliced fresh mushrooms
- 4 large eggs – select organic when available
- 1 tbsp. extra virgin olive oil
- Knorr® Hollandaise Sauce Mix

PREPARATION:

1. In a small colander, rinse and drain asparagus. Break asparagus into bite size pieces, discarding woody stalks. Rinse spinach well, and set aside.
2. Steam asparagus in covered steamer basket for 3 to 5 minutes over medium heat until asparagus is crisp-tender or to taste.
3. Coat the cooking surface of a two inch deep skillet with 1/2 tbsp. olive oil. Add water to within one inch of rim. Preheat over high until water simmers.
4. Crack eggs and slowly release egg white and yolk into simmering water. Cover skillet and reduce heat to very low.
5. Prepare Hollandaise Sauce according to package directions. Set aside.
6. Coat a large skillet with 1/2 tbsp. olive oil. Add mushrooms, cover, and cook over medium-low heat for about 4 minutes, stirring occasionally until mushrooms brown slightly and release their juices.

7. Add the coarsely chopped spinach, cover, and cook for about 1 more minute, until the spinach begins to wilt.

8. Warm the crabmeat in a small skillet over low heat for one minute. Place half on top of each piece of toast.

9. Poach the eggs to desired doneness (about 15 minutes) and place 2 on top of each slice of toast.

10. Arrange half of asparagus on each plate on one side of egg covered crabmeat.

11. Arrange spinach and mushroom mixture on top of each serving.

12. Spoon Hollandaise sauce over top of spinach and mushroom mixture. Bon Appetite'!

NOT TOO BASIC VEGETARIAN BREAKFAST BURRITO TO GO

YIELD:

Per portion:

GI: 30
GL: 6

CALORIES: 501; Carbohydrates: 20g; Fiber: 11g; Protein: 29.5g; Fat: 31g; Saturated Fats: 23g; Sodium: 743mg

INGREDIENTS:

- 1/3 cup Lightlife® Smart Ground® Mexican Style seasoned veggie protein crumbles
- 1 oz. cheddar cheese, shredded
- 1 Mission® Carb Balance® Small Whole Wheat Tortilla
- 1 fresh extra-large egg and one egg white
- 1 tbsp. organic coconut oil

PREPARATION:

1. Coat cooking surface of medium sized skillet with coconut oil and preheat skillet over medium heat.
2. Add Smart Ground® to skillet. Cook and stir over medium heat for 4 to 6 minutes, breaking up crumbles.
3. In a small bowl, whisk egg and egg white well. Pour egg mixture into skillet.
4. Add 1 oz. shredded cheddar cheese.
5. Cook entire mixture to desired doneness.
6. Place tortilla in a moist paper towel, and microwave on high setting for 30 seconds.
7. Remove tortilla from paper towel. Place tortilla on a piece of parchment paper cut to just a bit larger in size than the tortilla.

8. Place cooked mixture in middle of tortilla. Fold up one end of tortilla to cover part of filling. Tuck in one side of tortilla, and roll up to enclose entire filling.
9. Fold up an end of the parchment paper. Roll up tortilla in parchment paper. Enjoy on your journey.

SCRAMBLED EGGS ON GARLIC WHEAT WITH MOZZARELLA TOMATO

YIELD: Serves 2

Per portion:

GI: 51
GL: 9.84

CALORIES: 356; Carbohydrates: 19.29; Fiber: 2g; Protein: 19.5g; Fat: 29g; Saturated Fats: 8g; Sodium: 415mg

INGREDIENTS:

- 4 extra-large eggs
- 1/4 cup purified water
- 1/8 tsp. freshly ground peppercorns, to taste
- 1 slice 100% Whole Grain Bread (produced by Natural Ovens®, USA)
- 2 one ounce slices ripe tomato
- 2 oz. part skim mozzarella cheese, shredded
- 2 tsp. olive oil
- 1 clove fresh garlic, peeled

PREPARATION:

1. Break the eggs into a bowl, add the water, salt and pepper and beat lightly until just mixed.
2. Coat cooking surface of a large skillet with olive oil, preheat skillet over medium heat.
3. Reduce heat to medium-low, add the beaten eggs, cover, and cook for about 1 minute. Using a spoon, gently stir until the egg is thoroughly cooked. Cover skillet to keep eggs warm and turn off the heat.
4. Place tomatoes on pan under broiler until they begin to wrinkle. Top each with ¼ of mozzarella cheese. Broil about 2 minutes more, until cheese melts.

5. Toast the bread. Briskly rub the peeled garlic clove over the toast, leaving as much garlic residue as possible on the toasted bread.
6. Slice the bread in half diagonally and place each half on a separate serving plate. Divide the scrambled eggs equally onto each serving of toasted bread and serve immediately with half of mozzarella topped grilled ripe tomato slices on the side.

YIPPIE YI YAY - SATISFYING SOUTHWESTERN SCRAMBLE

YIELD: Serves 2

Per portion:

GI: 40
GL: 2.50

CALORIES: 330; Carbohydrates: 6.25g; Fiber: 2g; Protein: 13.75g; Fat: 22g; Saturated Fats: 11.50g; Sodium: 312mg

INGREDIENTS:

- 4 Oscar Mayer® low-sodium thin bacon strips
- 2 tbsp. of fat-free sour cream
- 1/4 cup of onion, chopped
- 1/2 cup green pepper, chopped
- 2 fresh extra-large eggs
- 1 tbsp. Tabasco® Sauce
- 2 tbsp. unsalted organic butter

PREPARATION:

1. In a medium sized skillet, fry bacon until crisp over medium heat. Place crisp bacon on a paper towel on a small plate. Cover and set aside. Remove bacon grease from skillet.
2. Break eggs into a medium sized mixing bowl. Beat with spoon until frothy.
3. Add onion, green pepper, and sour cream. Mix well.
4. Spread butter over cooking surface of skillet and preheat over medium heat.
5. Pour in egg and vegetable mixture. Stir eggs until cooked to desired consistency.
6. Remove eggs to warm platter. Sprinkle with southwest seasoning.

SOME LIKE IT SPICY EGGS

YIELD: Serves 4

Per portion:

GI: 40
GL: 2.61

CALORIES: 146.25; Carbohydrates: 6.54g; Fiber: 2g; Protein: 7g; Fat: 9.5g; Sat. Fat: 2.5; sodium: 74.12 mg

INGREDIENTS:

- 1 cup chopped red bell pepper
- 1/4 cup chopped sweet onion
- 1 tsp. minced garlic
- 1/2 tsp. cayenne pepper
- 4 fresh extra-large eggs
- Handful of fresh cilantro (select 4 nice sprigs)
- 1 tbsp. extra virgin olive oil

PREPARATION:

1. Combine first 5 ingredients in mixing bowl.
2. Whisk for two minutes.
3. Coat cooking surface of medium sized skillet with olive oil, and preheat skillet over medium heat.
4. Pour egg mixture into pan.
5. Continue to stir as this will cook together quickly.
6. When eggs are fully cooked, divide spicy eggs and vegetables equally among 4 warm serving plates and top each serving with a sprig of fresh cilantro.

SAVORY SUNRISE OMELET

YIELD: Serves 1

Per portion:

GI: 40
GL: 8.18

CALORIES: 360; Carbohydrates: 20.47; Fiber: 4g; Protein: 28g; Fat: 18g; Saturated Fats: 6g; Sodium: 572mg

INGREDIENTS:

- 1/2 cup red bell pepper, chopped
- 1/4 cup 2% milk reduced fat cheddar cheese, shredded
- 1/2 cup chopped onion
- 1/2 cup egg substitute
- 1/8 tsp. freshly ground black peppercorns, to taste
- 1 tbsp. extra virgin olive oil

PREPARATION:

1. Coat cooking surface of medium sized pan with olive oil and preheat over medium heat.
2. Pour egg substitute into pan. Add freshly ground black peppercorns, to taste. With a spatula, lift edges of eggs, allowing uncooked portions to flow underneath until all eggs are set.
3. Turn eggs over like a pancake.
4. Add onion, bell pepper, and top with cheese.
5. Reduce heat to low, and cook for one minute until cheese melts. Fold in half and remove to warm serving plate.

MAURY STYLE SUPER SMOOTHIE

YIELD: Serves 1

Per portion:

GI: 44
GL: 9.50

CALORIES: 316; Carbohydrates: 21.59g; Fiber: 4.7g; Protein: 27.36g; Fat: 15g; Saturated Fats: 7g; Sodium: 472mg

INGREDIENTS:

- 8 oz. Unsweetened Blue Diamond® Almond Breeze®
- 4 oz. The Greek Gods® Traditional Plain Yogurt
- 1 level scoop Lifetime® Life's Basics® Plant Protein Powder (1.24 oz.) Natural Vanilla Flavor
- 2 oz. Del Monte® canned peaches, packed in 100% juice
- 2 drops almond extract

PREPARATION:

1. Place ingredients in blender. Cover.
2. Blend at high speed for 30 seconds. Enjoy.

ASTA LA VISTA SUPREME

YIELD: Serves 1

Per portion:

GI: 50
GL: 10

CALORIES: 424.50; Carbohydrates: 20g; Fiber: 10.50g; Protein: 29.36g; Fat: 25.25g; Saturated Fats: 5.93g; Sodium: 534mg

INGREDIENTS:

- 1 Mission® Carb Balance® Small Whole Wheat Tortilla
- 2 ounces 95% lean ground beef, cooked, drained, and warm
- 1 oz. diced avocado
- 1 tbsp. fat-free sour cream,
- 1 oz. red, ripe tomato, diced
- 1 tbsp. black olives, sliced
- 1 tbsp. fat free refried beans
- 2 large egg whites
- 1 tbsp. organic coconut oil

PREPARATION:

1. Coat the cooking surface of a medium sized skillet with coconut oil.
2. Preheat skillet over medium heat. Whisk egg whites in a small bowl. Pour egg whites into preheated skillet and cook to taste.
3. Heat refried beans in microwave oven on high power for 30 seconds. Stir. Continue heating on high power for another 30 seconds.
4. Wrap tortilla in moist paper towel. Cook tortilla in microwave on high power for one minute. Remove paper towel and place tortilla on serving dish.
5. Place ground beef, fat-free sour cream, diced avocado, tomato, olives, refried beans, and egg on top of the tortilla.

SOME LIKE IT HOT SPINACH TOFU CURRY

YIELD: Serves 2

Per portion:

GI: 50
GL: 9.43

CALORIES: 283.5; Carbohydrates: 18.86g; Fiber: 3.28+g; Protein: 13.66g; Fat: 13.98g; Saturated Fats: 3.88g; Sodium: 523.5mg

INGREDIENTS:

- 3/4 cup diced onion
- 1 cup rinsed, chopped fresh spinach
- 6 oz. Mori-Nu® Silken Firm Tofu, pressed and crumbled
- 1 cup diced fresh red ripe tomatoes
- 2 oz. reduced fat shredded cheddar cheese
- 3 cloves fresh minced garlic
- 1 tbsp. extra virgin olive oil
- 1 tsp. curry powder
- 1/4 tsp. cayenne pepper
- 1 tsp. cumin
- 1 tsp. turmeric
- 1/8 tsp. freshly ground black peppercorns, to taste

PREPARATION:

1. Coat cooking surface of medium sized skillet with olive oil.
2. Place skillet over medium heat, and sauté the onion and garlic for about 3 minutes until the onion becomes soft.
3. Add the remaining ingredients except the spinach, stirring frequently for an additional 3 ½ to 5 minutes, until tofu is well heated.

4. Add spinach, cover and heat over very low heat for just a minute or two until spinach just begins to wilt.
5. Divide equally onto 2 serving plates, and serve immediately.

EUROPEAN VEGGIE OMELET

YIELD: Serves 1

Per portion:

GI: 40
GL: 7.20

CALORIES: 502.13; Carbohydrates: 18g; Fiber: 4.75g; Protein: 22g; Fat: 38.75g; Saturated Fats: 8.25g; Sodium: 291.88mg

INGREDIENTS:

- 1/4 cup mushroom, diced
- 1/4 cup onion, diced
- 1/4 cup green pepper, diced
- 1/4 cup tomato, diced
- 1 oz. almonds, chopped
- 1 oz. Jarlesberg® Reduced Fat Swiss cheese, shredded
- 1 fresh extra-large egg
- 1 tbsp. skim milk
- 1 tbsp. extra virgin olive oil

PREPARATION:

1. In a medium size bowl, whisk together egg and milk for a minute.
2. Add green pepper, onion, tomato, mushrooms, and mix well.
3. Coat cooking surface of medium sized skillet with olive oil. Preheat skillet over medium heat.
4. Pour in egg, milk, and vegetable mixture.
5. Reduce heat to low, cover with a lid and cook for about 3 minutes until egg is set to desired consistency.
6. Sprinkle Swiss cheese on top. Turn off the heat.
7. Allow to stand covered for about a minute, allowing cheese to melt.
8. Sprinkle with chopped almonds and enjoy.

MOUTH WATERING STEAK AND EGGS

YIELD: Serves 1

Per portion:

GI: 40
GL: 2.13

CALORIES: 653; Carbohydrates: 13.33g; Fiber: 4g; Protein: 42g; Fat: 41g; Saturated Fats: 14g; Sodium: 130mg

INGREDIENTS:

- 3 ounces cooked lean beef tenderloin
- 1/2 cup sliced red bell pepper
- 1/2 cup sliced onion
- 2 fresh extra-large eggs
- 1 tbsp. extra virgin olive oil
- 1 tbsp. unsalted organic butter

PREPARATION:

1. Coat the cooking surface of a skillet with olive oil.
2. Preheat skillet over medium heat, and add red bell pepper and onion. Cover skillet; stir gently occasionally, adding water if needed to keep vegetables from sticking.
3. Cook vegetables until just tender, for about 3 minutes or to taste.
4. Remove vegetables from skillet and set aside, covering to keep them warm.
5. Whisk eggs together in a small bowl until well mixed.
6. Pour eggs into skillet and cook over medium heat until eggs are thoroughly cooked. Move eggs to one side of skillet, and turn off the heat.
7. Place beef sirloin tips and butter into skillet. Cover the skillet to allow heat to gently warm beef sirloin tips (for about a minute). Mix beef tips to coat with butter.
8. Assemble onto serving plate and enjoy!

ORIENT TENDERLOIN ROLL TO GO

YIELD: Serves 2

Per portion:

GI: 40
GL: 9.48

CALORIES: 438.75; Carbohydrate: 23.7g; Fiber: 10.62g; Protein: 42.67g; Fat: 16g; Saturated Fats: 4.5g; Sodium: 635.5mg

INGREDIENTS:

- 6 ounces pork tenderloin, sliced into ½ inch thick pieces
- 1 cup chopped red bell pepper
- 3/4 cup chopped onion
- 1/2 tsp. Tamari® Reduced Sodium Soy Sauce
- 1/2 tsp. Bragg® Liquid Aminos
- 1 cup egg substitute
- 1 tbsp. extra virgin olive oil
- 1 tbsp. minced fresh garlic
- 2 Mission® Carb Balance® Small Whole Wheat Tortillas

PREPARATION:

1. Cover the cooking surface of a medium skillet with olive oil. Add pork tenderloin, minced garlic, low sodium soy sauce, and Bragg® Liquid Aminos. Cover, and allow mixture to marinade for about 10 minutes to tenderize the pork tenderloin. You may refrigerate overnight if you prefer.
2. When you are ready to prepare this dish, place the skillet over medium heat. Cook, covered for about 20 minutes, stirring as needed to keep pork from sticking. You may add a bit of water, if necessary.
3. Add the chopped onion and red bell pepper, and cook for another 10 minutes, until the vegetables are crisp-tender. (You may need to add a bit of water.)

4. Remove the pork tenderloin and vegetable mixture to a warm, covered dish to keep warm.
5. Pour eggs into the skillet, and cook over medium heat, stirring occasionally until the eggs are set. Turn off the heat, and cover to keep warm.
6. Warm the tortillas in a microwave wrapped in a moist towel on high heat for 1 minute. Remove tortilla from paper towel and place on parchment paper.
7. Place half of the pork tenderloin mixture and half of the scrambled egg mixture on each tortilla. Fold over one end of each tortilla, and then roll up each tortilla. Fold one end of the parchment paper over rolled tortilla, roll up parchment paper as you did the tortilla, and you are ready to serve and go.

CANADIAN BACON AND BETTER'N EGGS®

YIELD: Serves 1

Per portion:

GI: 40
GL: 4.8

CALORIES: 332; Carbohydrate: 12g; Fiber: 1g; Protein: 38g; Fat: 1890g; Saturated Fats: 5g; Sodium: 901mg

INGREDIENTS:

- 3 slices Jones® Naturally Hickory Smoked sliced Canadian Bacon
- 1/2 cup Better'n Eggs® egg substitute
- 1/2 cup chopped onion
- 1 oz. reduced fat mild cheddar cheese, shredded
- 1 tbsp. extra virgin olive oil

PREPARATION:

1. Coat the cooking surface of a small skillet with olive oil, and place over medium heat.
2. Add the Canadian bacon slices, and heat to desired temperature. Remove to a heated, covered plate.
3. Place chopped onion into skillet, cover, and cook until slightly browned.
4. You can add a little water to the skillet, if desired.
5. Pour the egg substitute into the skillet, and cook until set, stirring as desired. Sprinkle with shredded low-fat Cheddar cheese. Cover and turn off heat. Allow skillet to rest for about a minute until cheese melts.

TEMPEH JACK

YIELD: Serves 2

Per portion:

GI: 50
GL: 6.26

CALORIES: 428; Carbohydrates: 12.51g; Fiber: 2.9g; Protein: 25.29g; Fat: 15.83g; Saturated Fats: 12.85g; Sodium: 356.5mg

INGREDIENTS:

- 4 oz. tempeh, crumbled
- 2 fresh extra-large eggs
- 2 oz. sliced leek
- 2 oz. avocado slices
- 2 oz. sliced red bell pepper
- 2 oz. shredded Monterey Jack cheese
- 2 tbsp. picante sauce (Pace®)
- 1 tbsp. extra virgin olive oil

PREPARATION:

1. Coat cooking surface of skillet with olive oil and preheat over medium heat.
2. Add tempeh to skillet and brown slightly, stirring occasionally for about four minutes.
3. In a small bowl, whisk eggs until frothy while tempeh is cooking.
4. Add red bell pepper and leek to the skillet with the tempeh, cooking until vegetables are tender, for about another minute, stirring occasionally.
5. Add eggs to skillet with vegetables. Continue to cook, stirring occasionally, until eggs are completely set, for about another minute. Spread scrambled egg and vegetable mixture evenly over cooking surface of skillet.
6. Sprinkle shredded cheese evenly on top of the cooked tempeh, egg, and vegetable mixture.

7. Turn off the heat and place a cover over the skillet allowing the cheese to melt, for about another minute.
8. Distribute tempeh, egg, and vegetable mixture equally onto two serving plates.
9. Place half of avocado slices on each plate.
10. Top each serving with 1 tbsp. of picante sauce.

BETTER'N EGGS® AND BACON BURRITO

YIELD: Serves 1

Per portion:

GI: 40
GL: 9.60

CALORIES: 406; Carbohydrates: 24g; Fiber: 10g; Protein: 27g; Fat: 24g; Saturated Fats: 19.57.5g; Sodium: 837mg

INGREDIENTS:

- 2 slices Oscar Mayer® Low Sodium Bacon, cooked and drained on a paper towel
- 1 oz. low sodium cheddar cheese, shredded
- 1/2 cup chopped onion
- 1/2 cup Better'n Eggs® egg substitute
- 1 tbsp. organic coconut oil
- 1 Mission® Carb Balance® Small Whole Wheat Tortilla

PREPARATION:

1. Coat cooking surface of medium sized skillet with 1 tbsp. coconut oil. Preheat skillet over medium heat.
2. Add chopped onion, cover, cooking to desired doneness. You can add a bit of water so onion doesn't stick and burn.
3. Add Better'n Eggs® to skillet, cooking gently until eggs are set.
4. Top eggs with 1 oz. shredded cheddar cheese.
5. Cover, turn off the heat, and allow cheese to melt (for about a minute).
6. Place the tortilla in a moist paper towel and microwave at high power for one minute.
7. Remove paper towel and place tortilla on a plate. Place bacon, Better'n Eggs® and onion mixture on warmed tortilla, fold tortilla in half to cover filling and enjoy.

ORIENTAL BREAKFAST CREPES'

YIELD: Serves 4

Per portion:

GI: 40
GL: 5.30

CALORIES: 438.5; Carbohydrate: 13.25g; Fiber: 5.13; Protein: 35.61g; Fat: 25g; Saturated Fats: 7g; Sodium: 328.75mg

INGREDIENTS:

- 3/4 pound 90% lean ground sirloin, cooked
- 2 cups thinly sliced Brussels sprouts
- 1 cup shredded carrots
- 6 fresh extra-large eggs, organic preferred
- 3/4 cup thinly sliced scallions (10 – 12)
- 1 tbsp. Bragg® Liquid Aminos
- 2 tbsp. ground raw flaxseed
- 1/2 cup chopped red bell pepper
- 2 tbsp. extra virgin olive oil
- 1 tbsp. minced garlic
- 1 tbsp. grated fresh ginger
- 4 tbsp. water

PREPARATION:

1. Cover the cooking surface of an electric wok or skillet with 1 tbsp. olive oil.
2. Add Bragg® Liquid Aminos, 2 tbsp. water, Brussels sprouts, carrots, ginger, red bell pepper, and minced garlic, stirring to combine and coat vegetables with liquid. Cover, and allow vegetables to marinade for about 5 minutes.
3. When you are ready to prepare this dish, heat wok to 300 degrees or place skillet over low-medium heat.

4. Cover and cook vegetable mixture for about 7 minutes, stirring occasionally and adding water as needed to keep vegetables from sticking until they become tender and slightly browned or to taste. Remove vegetables from wok, set vegetables aside and cover to keep warm.
5. In a medium sized mixing bowl, whisk eggs, 2 tbsp. water, minced garlic and ginger.
6. Coat the same cooking surface again with 1 tsp. olive oil.
7. Preheat wok or skillet over medium heat.
8. Gently ladle one fourth of egg mixture (5 tbsp.) onto cooking surface.
9. After half a minute, carefully lift edges with a spatula, tilting pan to allow egg mixture to flow underneath.
10. Cover and cook for another minute or two, until eggs are firmly set.
11. Top with 3 oz. 90% lean ground sirloin. Turn off the heat. Replace cover, and let rest for 30 seconds to warm sirloin.
12. Spread one fourth of the vegetable mixture on top, and sprinkle with 1 ½ tsp. ground flaxseed.
13. Remove crepe to serving plate.
14. Repeat from #6 above for the remaining three Oriental Crepes.

FESTIVAL FLORENTINE

YIELD: Serves 2

Per portion:

GI: 55
GL: 9.09

CALORIES: 280.5; Carbohydrate: 16.53g; Fiber: 4.05; Protein: 16.62g; Fat: 19.34g; Saturated Fats: 5.95g; Sodium: 409mg

INGREDIENTS:

- 4 oz. fresh spinach, steamed and squeezed dry
- 2 oz. fresh avocado slices
- 2 one oz. slices fresh ripe tomato
- 2 oz. low fat mild cheddar cheese, shredded
- 2 extra-large hard boiled eggs, thinly sliced
- 1 slice Healthy Choice 7 Grain bread (Con Agra, USA), lightly toasted
- 2 tbsp. low sodium mayonnaise
- 1 tbsp. unsalted organic butter

PREPARATION:

1. Place toasted bread slice on toaster oven pan. Spread toast slice with 1 tbsp. butter.
2. Cut bread in half diagonally. Sprinkle each half with an ounce of shredded cheddar cheese.
3. Place 2 oz. steamed spinach on each piece of bread, and then top with a tomato slice.
4. Arrange egg slices on top of tomato slices, using one egg for each piece of bread.
5. Top each egg with a tbsp. of mayonnaise, spreading mayonnaise slightly, to partially cover the egg slices.

6. Broil for 2 to 3 minutes, until mayonnaise just begins to brown slightly.
7. Top each Florentine with 1 oz. of fresh avocado slices.
8. Place each serving onto a warm serving plate.

ZUCCHINI OMELET

YIELD: Serves 1

Per portion:

GI: 40
GL: 3.85

CALORIES: 312.63; Carbohydrate: 9.62g; Fiber: 3.125g; Protein: 25g; Fat: 18.5g; Saturated Fats: 12.5g; Sodium: 680.5mg

INGREDIENTS:

- 1/2 cup sliced zucchini
- 1 tbsp. chopped green pepper
- 1 oz. chopped onion
- 1/8 tsp. dried oregano, thyme, or marjoram or a mix of all three
- 1/2 cup egg substitute
- 1 tbsp. grated parmesan cheese
- 1 oz. part skim mozzarella cheese
- 2 tsp. finely chopped fresh parsley
- 1 tsp. unsalted organic butter

PREPARATION:

1. Coat a medium sized skillet with butter, and preheat over medium heat. (As an alternative, you may add a little water to the pan and "no-oil" cook the vegetables if you prefer.)
2. Add the zucchini, peppers, onions and herbs to the preheated pan.
3. Cook the vegetable mixture, stirring occasionally, for about 2 minutes, until the vegetables are crisp/tender to taste.
4. Remove the vegetable mix from the pan and place on a small, covered dish to keep warm.
5. Recoat the skillet with a 1/3 second spray of canola oil cooking spray and place over medium-low heat.

6. Add the egg substitute and cook, without stirring, until the mixture becomes set at the edges.
7. Flip with a spatula, allowing the un-cooked portion of the eggs to cook for 1 more minute, or until almost set.
8. Place vegetable mixture and the cheeses on the omelet, cover, reduce heat to very low and allow the cheese to melt, for about one minute.
9. Slide the omelet onto a serving plate and garnish with fresh parsley.

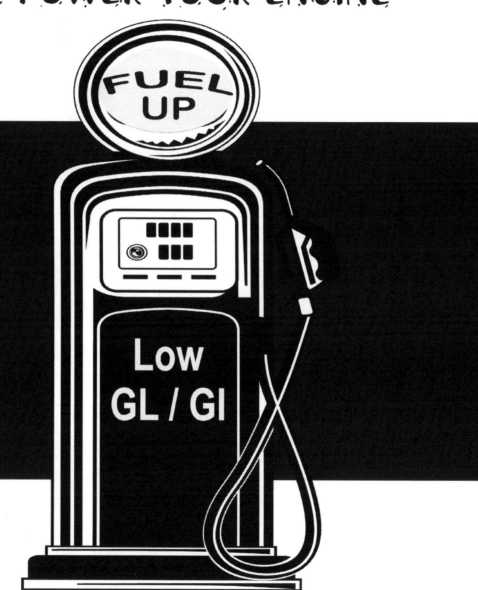

FISHERMAN'S LUNCH

YIELD: Serves 2

Per portion:

GI: 50
GL: 9.94

CALORIES: 385.5; Carbohydrates: 19.88g; Fiber: 9.38g; Protein: 24g; Fat: 29g; Saturated Fats: 5g; Sodium: 4217.25mg

INGREDIENTS:

- 2 large hardboiled eggs, peeled and sliced
- 4.25 oz. can of sardines in oil, drained
- 4 oz. avocado, cubed
- 1/2 head of romaine lettuce
- 8 oz. fresh tomato, deseeded, sliced into wedges
- 1/2 cup cucumber, deseeded, sliced into 1/2 inch strips
- 1/4 cup sweet purple onion, sliced
- 1/4 cup chopped fresh parsley
- 2 tbsp. Maries Raspberry Vinaigrette®
- 1 tbsp. extra virgin olive oil
- 1 tbsp. apple cider vinegar
- 1/4 tsp. freshly ground black peppercorns, to taste

PREPARATION:

1. Combine the olive oil, raspberry vinaigrette, apple cider vinegar, and ground black pepper in a jar, cover, shake vigorously, and place in refrigerator to chill for at least 20 minutes or overnight.
2. Rinse the romaine and parsley and gently pat dry.
3. Tear the romaine evenly divided into 2 salad bowls.
4. To each bowl, add an egg, half of the onion, parsley, avocado and tomato. Toss together gently.

5. Break each sardine into a few pieces and divide sardines evenly into each of the two salads.

6. Shake the dressing vigorously, then pour half over each salad. Place a cover over each bowl. Toss gently and serve immediately or keep salads chilled until ready to serve.

HEALTHFEST SALAD

YIELD: Serves 1

Per portion:

GI: 40
GL: 4.40

CALORIES: 426.5; Carbohydrates: 11g; Fiber: 7g; Protein: 18g; Fat: 33.17g; Saturated Fats: 6.5g; Sodium: 227.5mg

INGREDIENTS:

- 3 oz. "Fresh'N Easy Veggie Deluxe® Salad
- 2 oz. sliced avocado
- 1 oz. slice Jarlsberg® Lite Reduced fat Swiss cheese
- 1 tbsp. sunflower seeds, unsalted, dry roasted
- 1 tbsp. sliced red onion
- 1 tbsp. fresh lemon juice
- 1 tbsp. extra virgin olive oil
- 1 tbsp. apple cider vinegar
- 1 dash pepper sauce
- 1/2 tsp. freshly ground black peppercorns, to taste
- Sprig of fresh parsley

PREPARATION:

1. Mash the avocado in a small bowl with the lemon juice, pepper sauce and black pepper. Stir in the sunflower seeds. Top with cheese and onion.
2. Combine apple cider vinegar and olive oil in a small cup.
3. Arrange salad greens and red onion on salad plate.
4. Place avocado mixture in a rounded scoop on top of salad greens.
5. Pour apple cider vinegar and olive oil mixture on top of avocado mixture.
6. Garnish with sprig of fresh parsley.

HOT TUNA & RED PEPPER TORTILLA

YIELD: Serves 2

Per portion:

GI: 50
GL: 9.85

CALORIES: 487; Carbohydrates: 19.71g; Fiber: 6.1g; Protein: 32.48g; Fat: 27.85g; Saturated Fats: 5.5g; Sodium: 288.13mg

INGREDIENTS:

- 3/4 cup sweet red bell pepper, chopped
- 4 oz. plum tomatoes, sliced and deseeded
- 4.5 oz. can chunk light tuna canned in water without salt, drained
- 1/4 cup chopped sweet purple onion
- 2 tsp. minced garlic
- 4 extra-large eggs – select organic if available
- 2 tbsp. extra virgin olive oil
- 2 Mission® Carb Balance Whole Wheat Tortillas

PREPARATION:

1. Coat cooking surface of large sauté pan with 1 tbsp. olive oil and place over medium heat.
2. Place the red peppers in pan and sauté for about 3 minutes; add the onion and tomatoes and let simmer gently for about 2 minutes more, until vegetables are tender.
3. Add the drained tuna to this mixture, reduce heat to med-low setting, and continue cooking for about 2 minutes more, stirring gently occasionally.
4. Reduce heat to very low as juices from vegetables evaporate almost entirely.
5. While cooking the tuna and vegetables, whisk the eggs together in a medium size bowl.

6. Pour the cooked red peppers, onions, tomatoes and tuna into the bowl with the eggs and stir together.
7. Place the remaining tablespoon of olive oil in the sauté pan and preheat over medium heat.
8. Pour the egg and vegetable mixture into the preheated sauté pan.
9. Tilt sauté pan left and right quickly so mixture spreads and flows to cover all sides of cooking surface.
10. Reduce heat to low, allowing the egg mixture to gently cook.
11. Place a cover over the sauté pan and continue to cook over low heat until eggs become firmly set.
12. Wrap tortillas in moist paper towel and heat in microwave on high for one minute.
13. Remove tortillas from paper towel and place one tortilla on each serving plate.
14. When egg-vegetable tortilla is thoroughly cooked, slice in half, and slide each half onto a warm tortilla.
15. Fold up one end of each tortilla and carefully roll up to enclose the egg-vegetable mixture, using an oven mitt so as not to burn your hands.

CHICKEN, ASPARAGUS, AND BUTTER BEAN SALAD

YIELD: Serves 3

Per portion:

GI: 40
GL: 7.76

CALORIES: 286.33; Carbohydrates: 19.41g; Fiber: 3.58g; Protein: 30.33g; Fat: 6g; Saturated Fats: .33g; Sodium: 98.83mg

INGREDIENTS:

- 1 bag (about 6 cups) Fresh Express® 5 Lettuce Mix Salad Greens
- Three 4 oz. skinless, boneless chicken breast halves
- 1 cup freshly washed asparagus
- 1 cup canned butter beans, drained
- 1/4 cup apple cider vinegar
- 1 tbsp. freshly squeezed lemon juice
- 1 tbsp. Dijon mustard
- 1 tbsp. mayonnaise
- 1 tbsp. canola virgin olive oil
- 1 tbsp. fresh parsley, chopped
- 1/2 tbsp. fresh basil
- 1/2 tsp. freshly ground black pepper
- 1/4 tsp. paprika,
- 1 tsp. minced fresh garlic
- 1/2 tsp. chili powder

PREPARATION:

1. Preheat oven to 325 degrees.
2. Coat cooking surface of 8 X 11 inch baking dish with canola oil. Place chicken in baking dish. Sprinkle with parsley, basil, pepper, and paprika. Cover baking dish.
3. Bake chicken for 30 minutes in 325 degree oven.
4. While chicken is baking, prepare asparagus. Bend asparagus, three pieces at a time, until the tough ends snap off. Discard the ends.
5. Cook asparagus in a strainer basket resting over one inch of boiling water inside of a covered steamer pot for about 3 minutes, until crisp-tender or to taste.
6. Remove asparagus to a plate.
7. Distribute mixed greens evenly onto three serving plates. Add one third of both the asparagus and drained butter beans to the top of the salad greens on each plate. Place a cooked chicken breast on top of each salad.
8. Combine the lemon juice, chili powder, and garlic in a small mixing bowl; add the apple cider vinegar, mustard, and mayonnaise. Whisk ingredients together well. Pour 1/3 of the dressing over each of the three chicken salads and serve immediately.

GINGER LOVES CHICKEN BREAST WITH HEARTS OF ARTICHOKE

YIELD: Serves 1

Per portion:

GI: 40
GL: 3.60

CALORIES: 347; Carbohydrates: 9g; Fiber: 3g; Protein: 37g; Fat: 18g; Saturated Fats: 1g; Sodium: 129mg

INGREDIENTS:

- 4 oz. chicken breast
- 3 oz. artichoke hearts
- 1 oz. fresh ginger, very thinly sliced
- 1 oz. freshly squeezed lemon juice
- 1 tbsp. canola oil

PREPARATION:

1. Coat cooking surface of sauté pan with canola oil.
2. Place chicken breast, lemon juice and ginger in sauté pan and cover. Refrigerate for about 20 minutes while chicken absorbs marinade.
3. Place sauté pan over medium heat, and allow chicken to cook for about 10 minutes. Turn chicken over, cover, and cook for an additional 15 minutes, checking for doneness after about 10 minutes, and adding water as necessary to prevent chicken from sticking.
4. Chop artichoke hearts, large or small as you desire, place over chicken, cover and simmer for another minute to warm the hearts.
5. Remove chicken breast to serving plate, top with artichoke heart pieces.

JACK'S TURKEY BURGERS

YIELD: Serves 2

Per portion:

GI: 50
GL: 5.14

CALORIES: 282.63; Carbohydrates: 10.28g; Fiber: 1.38g; Protein: 21.5g; Fat: 16.25g; Saturated Fats: 3.5g; Sodium: 143.69mg

INGREDIENTS:

- 1/2 lb. ground turkey
- 1/2 cup finely chopped onion
- 2 oz. chopped portabella mushrooms
- 1/2 tbsp. chili powder
- 1/4 tsp. freshly ground black pepper
- 2 slices fresh red tomato, one oz. each
- 2 slices red onion, one oz. each
- 1 tbsp. extra virgin olive oil
- 2 outer leaves romaine lettuce, rinsed and dried well

PREPARATION:

1. Place the chopped onions, mushrooms, ground turkey, seasonings and spices in a large bowl. Mix well with clean hands. Form into 2 patties.
2. Coat cooking surface of medium sized skillet with olive oil, and preheat over medium heat.
3. Add turkey patties. Cook each patty about 7 minutes on each side, until done.
4. Place each burger on an outer leaf of romaine lettuce.
5. Top each burger with 1 slice of red onion, and 1 slice of tomato.

MINUTE STEAK SMOTHERED IN
MUSHROOM SAUCE

YIELD: Serves 4

Per portion:

GI: 40
GL: 1.40

CALORIES: 275; Carbohydrates: 3.5g; Fiber: .75g; Protein: 26.5g; Fat: 17g; Saturated Fats: 4.75g; Sodium: 13.25mg

INGREDIENTS:

- 1 pound of minute steaks – lean, thin cuts
- 1/2 pound sliced Portobello mushrooms
- 1/2 cup sliced onion
- 2 tbsp. extra virgin olive oil
- 1 tbsp. minced garlic
- 4 scallions, rinsed and chopped
- 4 tbsp. fresh parsley, rinsed and chopped
- 1/2 tsp. freshly ground black peppercorns, to taste

PREPARATION:

1. Coat cooking surface of large sauté pan with the olive oil and preheat over medium heat.
2. Place the minute steaks in preheated sauté pan.
3. Add chopped onion, sliced Portobello mushrooms, and minced garlic. Turn steaks after about a minute, and stir mushroom mixture. Cook for an additional minute, until steaks reach desired doneness.
4. Remove steaks to 4 warm serving plates.

5. Add 1/4 cup water to vegetable mixture in the sauté pan. Stir vegetable mixture until sauce begins to boil and vegetables are crisp-tender, or to taste.
6. Spoon vegetable and sauce mixture equally over the 4 servings of minute steak.
7. Sprinkle each serving equally with chopped scallions and chopped parsley.

PIXIE LEE'S CHICKEN

YIELD: Serves 2

Per portion:

GI: <1
GL: <1

CALORIES: 253; Carbohydrates: 14g; Fiber: 2.5g; Protein: 26.5g; Fat: 7g; Saturated Fats: 1g; Sodium: 990mg

INGREDIENTS:

- 2 boneless skinless chicken breasts, 4 oz. each
- 4 oz. organic Express® mixed salad greens
- 1 tbsp. extra virgin olive oil
- 1 tsp. low sodium soy sauce
- Juice of 1 fresh lemon
- 1 tsp. chili powder
- 1 tsp. ground cumin seeds
- 1 tsp. ground coriander seeds
- 1 tbsp. freshly minced garlic
- 1/4 cup red cooking wine
- 2 tbsp. chopped fresh cilantro
- 2 tbsp. of no-fat sour cream
- 1 lime, 2 inch diameter, sliced into wedges
- 1/4 cup water

PREPARATION:

1. Coat cooking surface of 8" X 8" glass baking dish with 1 tbsp. olive oil.
2. Mix together soy sauce, lemon juice, garlic and spices, in a medium bowl.
3. Place chicken breasts in baking dish. Pour soy sauce spice mixture over chicken breasts, being sure to coat all of chicken. Cover and refrigerate for 1 hour.
4. Preheat oven to 375 degrees.

5. Pour the cooking wine over the chicken breasts.
6. Bake, covered for 30 minutes, basting the chicken with the marinade juices every 10 minutes.
7. Place chicken evenly on 2 serving plates; put 1 tbsp. of sour cream on top of each chicken breast.
8. Add 1/4 cup water to baking dish. Stir to mix water with marinade mixture. Spoon 2 tbsp. sauce from baking dish onto the top of each chicken breast.
9. Serve each chicken breast with half of salad greens and half of lime wedges. Squeeze lime wedges over salad greens just before eating.

TEXAS STYLE SALMON CAESAR

YIELD: Serves 4

Per portion:

GI: 30
GL: 3.68

CALORIES: 414.25; Carbohydrates: 12.25g; Fiber: 2.75g; Protein: 33.88g; Fat: 16.87g; Saturated Fats: 1.38 g; Sodium: 154.88mg

INGREDIENTS:

- One pound (4) salmon fillets
- 4 cups inner leaves of romaine lettuce, rinsed and dried
- 4 tbsp. almond meal
- 1/2 cup plain low-fat skim milk yogurt
- 1/2 cup low sodium, low calorie mayonnaise
- 1/2 tsp. coriander
- 1/2 tsp. ground cumin seeds
- 1 oz. Jalapeno chilies, seeded and finely chopped (wear rubber gloves)
- 1 tsp. minced fresh garlic

PREPARATION:

1. Combine last 6 ingredients in a small mixing bowl. Whisk thoroughly to create Texas Mayonnaise.
2. Cover and refrigerate Texas Mayonnaise until ready to serve.
3. Rinse salmon and roll in almond meal, using 1 tbsp. per fillet.
4. Grill salmon fillets on a greased and preheated grill.
5. Cook, covered until fish flakes easily with a fork, about 12 minutes, turning fish once about half way through cooking.
6. Tear romaine lettuce and arrange on 4 serving plates.
7. Place a salmon fillet on top of each romaine lettuce bed.
8. Top each serving equally with 1/4 of Texas Mayonnaise.

TURKEY GARDEN BURRITO TO GO

YIELD: Serves 1

Per portion:

GI: 40
GL: 9

CALORIES: 415; Carbohydrate: 22.5g; Fiber: 9g; Protein: 33.50g; Fat: 20g; Saturated Fats: 8g; Sodium: 725.75mg

INGREDIENTS:

- 1/4 pound lean ground turkey
- 1 cup finely chopped fresh spinach
- 1 Mission® Carb Balance Small Whole Wheat Tortilla
- 2 oz. low-fat Monterey Jack cheese, shredded
- 1 clove fresh garlic, crushed
- 1/4 cup of minced onion
- 2 tbsp. Old El Paso® Mild Homestyle Salsa
- 1 tbsp. fat free sour cream
- 1 tbsp. sliced scallions
- 1 tbsp. black olives, sliced

PREPARATION:

1. Sauté the ground turkey with the minced garlic in a medium sized skillet over medium heat.
2. Cook, stirring occasionally, until the meat is no longer pink, and has a slightly toasted color, for about 15 minutes.
3. Reduce heat to low. Add the onions and the salsa, stirring occasionally for about 3 minutes until the onions begin to caramelize and soften.
4. When onions are cooked, add the chopped spinach to the skillet, cooking gently until spinach wilts slightly and excess liquid evaporates.

5. Wrap the tortilla in a moist paper towel and microwave on high for one minute.
6. Unwrap tortilla; place tortilla on parchment paper cut to just a bit larger in size than the tortilla. Add turkey mixture to center of tortilla.
7. Top turkey mixture with cheese, sour cream, scallions and olives.
8. Roll tortilla to form a burrito. Roll parchment paper around burrito to secure. Off you go, lunch in hand!

CHICKEN PROVOLONE WITH FRESH PESTO SAUCE

YIELD: Serves 2

Per portion:

GI: 30
GL: 1

CALORIES: 495; Carbohydrates: 3.5g; Fiber: .25g; Protein: 28g; Fat: 40.75g; Saturated Fats: 20.5g; Sodium: 375.25mg

INGREDIENTS:

- Two 3 oz. chicken breasts without skin
- 1/2 cup fresh basil leaves
- 2 tbsp. freshly grated Parmesan cheese
- 2 tbsp. extra virgin olive oil
- 1 tbsp. pine nuts, crushed
- 1 tbsp. minced fresh garlic
- 2 tbsp. extra virgin olive oil
- 2 one ounce slices Provolone cheese
- 2 sprigs fresh basil, for garnish

PREPARATION:

Prepare Pesto Sauce:

1. Place garlic, parmesan cheese, and pine nuts in blender. Pulse at high speed for several pulses to blend well and form a paste, scraping sides of blender as needed.
2. Add 1/2 cup fresh basil leaves, and pulse a few times to combine.

3. Add 2 tbsp. olive oil to the blender, alternately scrape of the sides of the blender with a spatula and then return blender to pulse in order to create a sauce. (If mixture is too thick, add 1 tbsp. water.)

Prepare Chicken:

1. Coat cooking surface of medium sized sauté skillet with olive oil, and pre-heat over medium heat.
2. Place fresh chicken breast in sauté pan, cover and cook for 10 minutes.
3. Remove cover and flip chicken breast over; cover and cook for another 10 minutes, or until chicken is thoroughly cooked. You can add a bit of water to prevent chicken from scorching.
4. Test with fork in center to make certain chicken is thoroughly cooked.
5. When chicken is fully cooked, add a slice of provolone cheese to the top of each chicken breast.
6. Scoop 1/2 of prepared pesto recipe onto the top of each slice of provolone cheese.
7. Cover pan, and turn off the heat. Let stand for two minutes, allowing provolone cheese to melt.
8. Garnish each breast with a sprig of fresh basil.
9. Divide equally onto 2 serving plates.

SAVORY SALMON SALAD

YIELD: Serves 2

Per portion:

GI: 40
GL: 4.40

CALORIES: 241.33; Carbohydrates: 11g; Fiber: 1.5g; Protein: 22.25g; Fat: 10.25g; Saturated Fats: .75g; Sodium: 763.75mg

INGREDIENTS:

- 7.5 oz. can salmon, well drained
- 2 cups rinsed and gently dried romaine lettuce pieces
- 1 tsp. minced fresh garlic
- 1 oz. freshly squeezed lemon juice
- 1 tsp. dry mustard
- 1 tsp. capers
- 2 tbsp. mayonnaise
- 2 tbsp. chopped purple onion
- 2 tbsp. chopped sweet red pepper
- 2 tbsp. chopped celery

PREPARATION:

1. Combine last 8 ingredients in a small mixing bowl.
2. Add salmon, and mix thoroughly.
3. Cover and chill several hours to develop flavor. (This can easily be prepared the evening before and refrigerated in a covered container for use the following day.)
4. Place 1 cup of romaine lettuce pieces on each of 2 serving plates.
5. Serve half of salmon mixture on each bed of romaine lettuce.

SUPERB SPAGHETTI SQUASH TENDERLOIN

YIELD: Serves 4

Per portion:

GI: 40
GL: <1

CALORIES: 294.25; Carbohydrates: 9.50g; Fiber: .75g; Protein: 35.75g; Fat: 4.25g; Saturated Fats: 2g; Sodium: 439.25mg

INGREDIENTS:

- 2 cups cooked spaghetti squash (See below for cooking instructions.)
- 2 cups Campbell's® Traditional Spaghetti Sauce
- 1 lb. pork tenderloin, cut into 1 inch cubes
- 1 cup sliced mushrooms
- 1/2 cup chopped onion
- 2 tbsp. minced garlic
- 1 tbsp. fresh oregano, finely chopped
- 1 tbsp. fresh thyme, finely chopped
- 1 tbsp. fresh basil, finely chopped
- 1 tbsp. cayenne pepper, or to taste
- 2 tbsp. extra virgin olive oil
- 1/2 cup water

PREPARATION:

1. Preheat oven to 350 degrees.
2. Coat cooking surface of a large water-tight skillet with 1 tbsp. olive oil, and preheat over medium heat.
3. Add pork tenderloin and 1/4 cup water. Cover skillet and cook tenderloin over medium heat for 35 minutes, stirring every 10 minutes to cook meat evenly. You can add more water as needed to prevent pork from sticking.
4. Cut the squash lengthwise and scoop out the seeds.

5. Coat surface of baking sheet with 1 tbsp. olive oil. Place squash on baking sheet cut side down.
6. Bake squash for thirty minutes or until the outer skin is easy to pierce with a fork.
7. When squash is through cooking, using a fork, scrape the squash from the outer skin to form strands that resemble spaghetti noodles and place 1/4 onto each serving plate.
8. After meat has cooked for 30 minutes, add mushrooms, onion, garlic, thyme, oregano, and basil.
9. Continue to cook, covered, over medium heat for another 10 minutes, stirring occasionally.
10. Add spaghetti sauce to meat mixture, and heat to boiling. Remove from heat and ladle 1/4 of meat and sauce mixture over each serving of spaghetti squash.

STIR-FRIED CHICKEN AND VEGETABLES IN TORTILLA WRAPS

YIELD: Serves 2

Per portion:

GI: 40
GL: 8.60

CALORIES: 361; Carbohydrates: 21.5g; Fiber: 10.5g; Protein: 28.3g; Fat: 17g; Saturated Fats: 3.3g; Sodium: 984mg

INGREDIENTS:

- 2 small skinless, boneless chicken breast filets (about 7 oz.)
- 1 cup shredded cabbage
- 1 small red sweet pepper, thinly sliced
- 1/2 cup sugar snap peas, chopped diagonally
- 2 tbsp. peanut oil
- 2 tbsp. teriyaki sauce
- 1/2 tsp. freshly ground black peppercorns, to taste
- 2 Mission® Carb Balance Small Whole Wheat Tortillas

PREPARATION:

1. Trim any visible fat off the chicken breast filets, and cut into thin long strips.
2. Heat 1 tbsp. of oil in a medium pan over medium heat, tilting pan to coat surface.
3. Add the chicken strips, stirring continuously to make sure all sides of the chicken pieces brown slightly to keep the juices inside.
4. Reduce the heat and cook for 3 to 5 minutes until chicken is fully cooked. You can add a bit of water to keep chicken from sticking. When chicken is fully cooked, remove from pan and set aside on a plate. Cover to keep warm.

5. Add the remaining tablespoon of oil to the same pan; heat over medium heat and add all the vegetables. Stir fry the vegetables for 2-3 minutes, to taste. Do not overcook; the vegetables should still be slightly crunchy.

6. Return the cooked chicken strips to the pan. Add the teriyaki sauce and freshly ground black peppercorns, stirring well to coat chicken with all the ingredients.

7. Heat the tortillas in a moist paper towel in a microwave oven at high setting for one minute. Unwrap tortillas and place one on each serving plate.

8. Distribute chicken and vegetable mixture evenly over each of the 2 warm tortillas.

9. Fold over one end of each tortilla to enclose filling, and serve.

SOUTHWESTERN SALAD

YIELD: Serves 4

Per portion:

GI: 50
GL: 9.53

CALORIES: 294.88; Carbohydrates: 19.07g; Fiber: 4.63g; Protein: 34.63g; Fat: 7.92g; Saturated Fats: 3.63g; Sodium: 323.25mg

INGREDIENTS:

- 3/4 lb. lean ground beef (95%)
- 3/4 cup dried kidney beans, soaked, boiled without salt, and drained
- 1 cup fresh tomato, chopped and deseeded
- 1/2 cup shredded low-fat cheddar cheese
- 4 tbsp. fat free sour cream
- 4 tbsp. meatless bacon bits
- 4 outer leaves romaine lettuce, rinsed and patted dry
- 1 tbsp. chili powder
- 1/2 cup Old El Paso® Home-style Salsa

PREPARATION:

1. Brown ground beef in a large skillet over medium heat. Reduce heat and cook until beef is no longer pink, about 10 minutes. Remove beef from skillet, drain and blot with paper toweling to remove as much fat as possible.
2. Return beef to skillet. Add chili powder and beans to skillet. Continue to cook; stirring occasionally, until heated through, stirring well to combine chili powder into ground beef and bean mixture.
3. Arrange romaine lettuce leaves onto 4 serving plates.

4. Divide meat and bean mixture into four equal servings and spoon onto each of 4 large Romaine lettuce leaves.
5. Top each serving with 1/4 of each: chopped tomato, salsa, and shredded cheese.
6. Dress each serving with 1 tbsp. sour cream and 1 tbsp. bacon bits.

TOM'S TURKEY DIVINE

Yield: Serves 4

Per portion:

GI: 40
GL: 8.32

CALORIES: 463.81; Carbohydrates: 2.08g; Fiber: 4.5g; Protein: 49.13g; Fat: 23.78g; Saturated Fats: 11.40g; Sodium: 1186.88mg

INGREDIENTS:

- 3 cups cooked, skinless boneless turkey breast, cubed
- 2 cups broccoli flowerets, steamed until just tender
- 4 oz. Swiss cheese, shredded
- 1 cup Shelton's® Organic fat-free, Low Sodium Chicken Broth
- 1 cup chopped portabella mushrooms
- 1/4 cup additional Shelton's® Organic Fat-Free Low Sodium Chicken Broth
- 1/2 cup chopped onion
- 1/2 cup light whipping cream
- 1 tsp. soy lecithin granules
- 1/2 tsp. rubbed sage
- 1/4 tsp. marjoram leaves, crushed
- 1/4 cup grated parmesan cheese
- 1 tbsp. extra virgin olive oil
- 1/4 tsp. cayenne pepper and white pepper, to taste
- Canola oil cooking spray

PREPARATION:

1. Preheat oven to 350 degrees.
2. Spray a 6 X 10 inch baking dish for 1/3 second with canola oil cooking spray; arrange turkey cubes and broccoli in baking dish.

3. Coat cooking surface of medium sized skillet with olive oil and preheat over medium heat. Sauté onion and mushrooms for about 3 minutes until tender. You can add a bit of water to prevent vegetables from sticking.

4. Mix soy lecithin granules into 1/4 cup chicken broth in a small saucepan. Let stand for 10 minutes. Mix until smooth. Add 1/2 cup light whipping cream and 1 cup chicken broth, mixing to form a sauce.

5. Place saucepan over medium heat, and bring mixture to a boil, stirring constantly until sauce is somewhat thickened, about 1 minute.

6. Reduce heat; add herbs and Swiss cheese, stirring until cheese melts.

7. Add cayenne and white pepper to taste.

8. Pour sauce over turkey broccoli mixture.

9. Sprinkle with parmesan cheese.

10. Bake in 350 degree oven about 20 minutes, until bubbly.

11. Evenly divide onto 4 serving plates.

CRUNCHY TURKEY SANDWICH

YIELD: Serves 1

Per portion:

GI: 51
GL: 9.69

CALORIES: 410; Carbohydrates: 19g; Fiber: 11g; Protein: 37g; Fat: 21.5g; Saturated Fats: 5g; Sodium: 383mg

INGREDIENTS:

- 3 oz. cooked skinless turkey breast, sliced
- 1 slice 100% Whole Grain bread (Nature's Ovens®, USA)
- 1/2 tbs. low-fat mayonnaise
- 2 outer romaine lettuce leaves, rinsed and dried
- 1 slice tomato
- 1 slice Monterey Jack low-fat cheese
- 1 tbsp. sunflower seeds, roasted, unsalted
- 1 tbsp. alfalfa sprouts, rinsed and drained
- 1 tbsp. meatless bacon bits

PREPARATION:

1. Spread mayonnaise on slice of bread. Add bacon bits, turkey slices, cheese, alfalfa sprouts, slice of tomato, and sunflower seeds.
2. Top with romaine lettuce leaves.

SALMON DRESSED SCALLOP KABOBS

YIELD: Serves 6

Per portion:

GI: <1
GL: <1

CALORIES: 227.5; Carbohydrates: 3.75g; Fiber: 0g; Protein: 34.5g; Fat: 9.5g; Saturated Fats: .5g; Sodium: 747mg

INGREDIENTS:

- 12 oz. large sea scallops
- 12 oz. Fresh salmon, sliced into thin strips
- 3 tbsp. Tamari® Reduced Sodium soy sauce
- 2 tbsp. dry white cooking wine
- 1 – 2 drops liquid stevia
- 1 tbsp. grated fresh ginger
- 1 tbsp. extra virgin olive oil
- 6 bamboo skewers, soaked in water for 20 minutes

PREPARATION:

1. Combine Tamari® soy sauce, olive oil, cooking wine, stevia, and grated ginger in a medium size mixing bowl.
2. Add salmon strips and scallops. Stir to coat seafood with marinade mixture.
3. Cover and refrigerate for 30 minutes.
4. Drain seafood and reserve marinade.
5. Wrap scallops in salmon strips, and divide evenly onto the 6 bamboo skewers.
6. Preheat broiler. Place kabobs on a large oven-proof glass baking dish or aluminum foil.

7. Broil about 4 inches from heat for about 2-3 minutes.
8. Turn kabobs over, baste with reserved marinade, and continue to broil for an additional 2-3 minutes or until fish flakes easily with a fork.
9. Place 1 kabob on each of 6 serving plates.

MOM'S TURKEY MEATBALLS WITH YOGURT DILL SAUCE

Yield: Serves 4

Per portion:

GI: 40
GL: 2.72

CALORIES: 351.28; Carbohydrates: 6.81g; Fiber: .72g; Protein: 34.25g; Fat: 21.53g; Saturated Fats: 7.5g; Sodium: 50.41mg

INGREDIENTS:

- 1 pound low fat ground turkey
- 1 cup The Greek Gods® Greek Yogurt Traditional Plain (in the green container)
- 1/2 cup very finely diced onion
- 2 tsp. freshly squeezed lemon juice
- 1 ½ tsp. very finely chopped fresh dill
- 1 ¼ cup chopped fresh parsley
- 1 tsp. minced fresh garlic
- 1/4 tsp. ground cloves
- 1/4 tsp. chili powder
- 1/2 tsp. ground cinnamon
- 1/2 tsp. freshly ground black peppercorns, to taste

PREPARATION:

1. Preheat oven to 350 degrees.
2. Combine 3 tbsp. yogurt, onion, lemon juice, parsley, minced garlic, cinnamon, cloves, and chili powder in a medium size mixing bowl.
3. Add ground turkey, and mix thoroughly to combine all ingredients.
4. Form mixture into 20 meatballs, about 1 ¼ to 1 ½ inches in diameter.

5. Place in a shallow baking dish, and bake for about 12 minutes.
6. In a small mixing bowl, combine remaining yogurt, dill, and freshly ground black peppercorns to make sauce.
7. Turn Turkey meatballs over, and bake another 12 minutes. Remove from oven.
8. Separate meatballs in baking dish into 4 servings. Pour 1/4 of yogurt dill sauce over each 1/4 of baked turkey meatballs. Cover and allow sauce to heat over meatballs for about 2 minutes
9. Ladle meatballs and sauce evenly onto 4 serving dishes.

LONDON BROIL WITH SAUTEED MUSHROOMS

Yield: Serves 6

Per portion:

GI: 40
GL: 2.32

CALORIES: 288.58; Carbohydrates: 5.81; Fiber: 1.25g; Protein: 42.47; Fat: 8.17g; Saturated Fats: .67g; Sodium: 105.45mg

INGREDIENTS:

- One 1 ½ pound 1 inch thick London Broil
- 1/2 pound large fresh mushrooms
- 1/4 cup diced onion
- 3/4 cup diced onion
- 2 tsp. I Can't Believe It's Not Butter®
- 2 tsp. Newman's Own® Teriyaki marinade
- 2 tbsp. minced fresh garlic
- 1 tbsp. ground mustard seed
- 1 tbsp. extra virgin olive oil
- 1/2 tsp. freshly ground black peppercorns, to taste

PREPARATION:

1. In a medium size mixing bowl, combine 1/4 cup diced onion, teriyaki marinade, ground mustard seed, and minced garlic.
2. Add London broil to marinade mixture, stirring to coat all surfaces of meat. Cover and refrigerate for an hour or overnight.
3. Broil or charbroil meat for about 5 minutes on each side, until it becomes medium-rare; coating with reserved marinade mixture half way through cooking.

4. While meat is cooking, sauté 3/4 cup onion and mushrooms in olive oil in a medium sized skillet until vegetables are tender. You can add a bit of water and cover to avoid sticking.
5. Remove meat from broiler; set aside for 5 minutes.
6. Slice thinly across the grain.
7. Distribute meat evenly among 6 serving plates, and top each serving with 1/6 of the sautéed mushroom and onion mixture.

SPINACH STUFFED TURKEY BREAST

YIELD: Serves 6

Per portion:

GI: 40
GL: 3.56

CALORIES: 237; Carbohydrates: 8.91g; Fiber: .42g; Protein: 29.5g; Fat: 6.5g; Saturated Fats: 2.66g; Sodium: 1215.67mg

INGREDIENTS:

- 1 ¾ pounds boneless turkey breast tenderloins
- 8 oz. Fresh spinach leaves, washed, with stems removed
- 1 cup part skim ricotta cheese
- 1/2 cup chopped onion
- 1 extra-large egg
- 1 oz. roasted red hot chili pepper; fresh or bottled, finely chopped in food processor (Do not touch with bare hands.)
- 1 tbsp. minced fresh garlic
- 2 tbsp. extra virgin olive oil, separated
- 1 tsp. dried rosemary

PREPARATION:

1. Preheat oven to 325 degrees.
2. Slice tenderloins in half lengthwise through the thickest part; season with pepper.
3. Put ricotta, egg, spinach, onion, and garlic in food processor. Pulse a few times to chop vegetables and combine ingredients.
4. Distribute spinach mixture evenly over turkey tenderloins.
5. Slice red pepper into strips, and arrange over spinach mixture.
6. Roll turkey around filling.
7. Tie rolls with a cotton string every few inches. (Or secure with toothpicks).

8. Coat glass baking dish with 1 tbsp. olive oil.
9. Arrange turkey rolls in baking dish; brush rolls with the remaining 1 tbsp. olive oil and top with rosemary.
10. Roast one hour, basting several times with liquid from roasting pan. When turkey is golden brown, cover baking dish and continue baking.
11. Remove string or toothpicks, cut into half inch slices, and top with juice from roasting pan.
12. Distribute evenly among 6 serving plates.

PORK CHOPS AND SAUERKRAUT

YIELD: Serves 4

Per portion:

GI: 40
GL: 7.60

CALORIES: 255; Carbohydrates: 19g; Fiber: 2.5g; Protein: 26g; Fat: 9g; Saturated Fats: 2.5g; Sodium: 365mg

INGREDIENTS:

- 1 ½ pounds center cut pork chops
- One 14 oz. can sauerkraut, rinsed and drained
- 1 cup The Greek Gods® Greek Yogurt Traditional Plain (in the green container)
- 1/2 cup thinly sliced onion
- 1 cup reconstituted frozen apple juice concentrate
- 1 tbsp. paprika
- 1/2 tsp. freshly ground black peppercorns, to taste
- 1 tbsp. extra virgin olive oil

PREPARATION:

1. Coat cooking surface of large skillet with olive oil and preheat over medium heat.
2. Add onion and sauté until lightly browned, for about one and one half minutes.
3. Remove onion to a large mixing bowl. Add sauerkraut, apple juice, and paprika, mixing well to combine all ingredients.
4. Sprinkle pork chops with freshly ground black peppercorns.
5. Brown pork chops in skillet over medium heat, about 4 minutes on each side.

6. Add sauerkraut mixture to pork chops in skillet. Cover tightly and simmer for 40 minutes over low heat, turning pork chops occasionally and basting with skillet liquids. Add a bit of water if it becomes dry.
7. Remove chops to 4 serving dishes.
8. Reduce heat to very low. Stir yogurt into sauerkraut mixture until it is just warmed – do not cook the yogurt.
9. Top 4 chops equally with yogurt-sauerkraut mixture.

GRILLED CHICKEN CAESAR SALAD

YIELD: Serves 2

Per portion:

GI: 40
GL: 1.70

CALORIES: 427.5; Carbohydrates: 4.25g; Fiber: .25g; Protein: 42.75g; Fat: 27.5g; Saturated Fat: 4; Sodium: 451mg

INGREDIENTS:

- 1/2 pound chicken breast fillets
- 1/2 cup Marie's® All Natural Caesar Dressing
- 2 tbsp. grated Parmesan cheese
- 2 tbsp. finely diced red onion
- 1 tsp. minced garlic
- 1/2 tsp. ground celery seed
- 1 large head romaine lettuce, separated, rinsed and dried

PREPARATION:

1. In a medium sized bowl, combine Marie's® All Natural Caesar Dressing, grated Parmesan cheese, finely diced red onion, minced garlic, and ground celery seed.
2. Marinade chicken for 30 minutes in half of marinade mixture, covered in refrigerator. Reserve other half of marinade mixture in small covered bowl in refrigerator for use as dressing.
3. Grill chicken until cooked thoroughly.
4. Place 2 large leaves of romaine lettuce cross-wise on each serving plate.
5. Slice remaining romaine into 2 inch strips, and divide evenly among both serving plates, placing romaine slices on top of large romaine leaves.
6. Top each lettuce pile with half of grilled chicken breast fillets.
7. Spoon reserved marinade mixture equally over each salad.

OVEN-FRIED CRISPY FISH

YIELD: Serves 4

Per portion:

GI: 38
GL: 7.22

CALORIES: 218.25; Carbohydrates: 19g; Fiber: 2.75 g; Protein: 30.25g; Fat: 3g; Saturated Fats: 1g; Sodium: 220.13mg

INGREDIENTS:

- 1 pound tilapia fillets
- 3 oz. Kellogg's All-Bran™ Flakes breakfast cereal (produced in Battlecreek MI, USA), finely ground in a food processor or blender
- Canola oil cooking spray
- 2 large eggs, whisked
- 3 tbsp. soy flour
- 1/2 tsp. freshly ground black peppercorns, to taste
- 1/4 tsp. paprika
- 1/4 tsp. Morton Lite Salt® Mixture
- 1/4 tsp. ground cayenne pepper
- 1 tsp. minced garlic
- 1/2 fresh lemon, sliced into 4 wedges
- 1 tbsp. freshly squeezed lemon juice

PREPARATION:

1. Coat a wire rack and large baking sheet by spraying for 1/3 second with canola oil cooking spray. Place the wire rack over the baking sheet.
2. Rinse fish fillets and blot dry with paper towels to remove excess moisture.
3. Position oven rack in the upper third of the oven.
4. Preheat oven to 425 degrees.
5. Place ground All-Bran In a shallow bowl and set aside.

6. In another shallow bowl, mix the soy flour, ground black peppercorns, paprika, Morton Lite Salt® Mixture, and minced garlic.
7. In a third shallow bowl, whisk together the eggs and lemon juice.
8. Dredge each fish fillet in the soy flour mixture, dip into egg mixture, and finally coat it with the breadcrumb and cereal mixture.
9. Spray all sides of the fish fillets lightly with a 1/3 second spray of canola oil cooking spray and arrange on the prepared wire rack.
10. Bake the fish fillets on the upper third oven rack in the preheated 425 degree oven for about 20 minutes, or until it flakes easily with a fork and the breading is golden brown.
11. Distribute fish evenly to 4 serving plates; garnish each serving with a fresh lemon wedge.

TERIYAKI BEEF BROCCOLI

YIELD: Serves 4

Per portion:

GI: 40
GL: 4.50

CALORIES: 333.88; Carbohydrates: 11.25g; Fiber: 6.25g; Protein: 39.13g; Fat: 11.5g; Saturated Fats: 4.5g; Sodium: 377mg

INGREDIENTS:

- 1 pound round steak of beef, trimmed of fat, sliced into thin strips
- 2 cups small broccoli florets
- 1 ½ cups fat-free, reduced sodium beef broth
- 1 cup thinly sliced onion
- 3/4 cup thinly sliced carrots
- 2 tbsp. reduced sodium teriyaki sauce
- 1 tbsp. very thinly sliced fresh ginger root
- 1 tbsp. extra virgin olive oil

PREPARATION:

1. Coat cooking surface of large skillet with olive oil, and preheat over medium heat.
2. Add beef and onions, and sauté until beef browns slightly, about 5 to 8 minutes.
3. Combine broth, teriyaki sauce, and gingerroot in a small mixing bowl.
4. Add broth mixture to skillet of beef, and bring to a boil.
5. Reduce heat to low and simmer, covered, until beef is just beginning to become tender, about 10 to 15 minutes.
6. Add carrots, and simmer for 5 minutes.
7. Add broccoli, and simmer for an additional 5 minutes.
8. Distribute evenly to 4 serving bowls.

LOW GLYCEMIC MEAT LOAF

YIELD: Serves 6

Per portion:

GI: 51
GL: 7.26

CALORIES: 222.83; Carbohydrates: 14.25g; Fiber: 3.42g; Protein: 25.58g; Fat: 7.33g; Saturated Fats: 3g; Sodium: 169.5mg

INGREDIENTS:

- 1 ½ pounds 95% lean ground beef
- 4 slices 100% Whole Grain Bread (produced by Natural Ovens®, USA), dried and grated
- 1 cup chopped onion
- 1/2 cup very finely chopped green bell pepper
- 1/2 cup Old El Paso® Medium Picante Salsa
- 1 extra-large egg, well beaten
- 1 tbsp. minced fresh garlic
- 1 tsp. cayenne pepper

PREPARATION:

1. Preheat oven to 350 degrees.
2. Combine last 7 ingredients in a large mixing bowl. Mix thoroughly.
3. Add ground beef, and mix very well.
4. Pat mixture into a 9" X 5" loaf pan.
5. Bake in 350 degree oven for an hour, until meat thermometer inserted in center registers 170 degrees and juices are clear.
6. Let stand in pan for 5 minutes; remove to serving platter.
7. Slice meatloaf into 6 equal portions.

MAURY'S CUSTOM CHILI

YIELD: 5 Servings

Per Portion:

GI: 40
GL: 9.62

CALORIES: 395.17; Carbohydrates: 24.05; Fiber: 6.7g; Protein: 38.2g; Fat: 13.9g; Saturated Fats: 8g; Sodium: 610.65mg

INGREDIENTS:

- 1 pound 95% lean ground beef
- 1 cup Eden® Organic Spicy Pintos
- 1 16 oz. can Rosarita® No Fat Refried Beans
- 4 ounces cheddar cheese, shredded
- 1/2 cup Chunky Salsa
- 1/2 cup chopped onion
- 2 tbsp. minced garlic
- 1 ¼ tsp. paprika
- 1 ¼ tsp. chili powder
- 1/4 tsp. thyme
- 2 tbsp. extra virgin olive oil

PREPARATION:

1. Coat cooking surface of large skillet with olive oil, and place over medium heat.
2. Add ground beef, stirring frequently as it cooks, to break into crumbles, for about 5 minutes. Remove from heat.
3. Transfer ground beef to a colander to drain grease. Press out excess moisture.
4. Return beef to skillet and place over low heat.

5. Immediately add pinto beans and their liquid, stirring to combine.
6. Add remaining ingredients.
7. Stir with a wooden spoon for 5 minutes over low heat, until bubbly.
8. Distribute evenly into 5 soup bowls.
9. Evenly divide shredded cheddar cheese onto the tops of each of the 5 servings.

GRAMMY'S VINTAGE VEAL BIRDS

YIELD: Serves 4

Per portion:

GI: 51
GL: 9.74

CALORIES: 359.31; Carbohydrates: 19.1g; Fiber: 2.38g; Protein: 24.75g; Fat: 20.44g; Saturated Fats: 5g; Sodium: 666.63mg

INGREDIENTS:

- 1 pound veal cutlets
- 2 slices 100% Whole Grain Bread (produced by Natural Ovens®, USA)
- One 10 ¾ oz. can Campbell's® Condensed 25% Less Sodium Cream of Mushroom soup
- 1/2 cup finely chopped onion
- 1 extra-large egg, well beaten
- 1 tbsp. minced fresh garlic
- Purified water to rinse bread
- 1 tbsp. extra virgin olive oil
- 1/4 cup nonfat milk

PREPARATION:

1. Preheat oven to 350 degrees.
2. Rinse bread slices, one at a time in cold water, squeezing out excess water. Place soaked bread slices in medium sized bowl.
3. Add egg to soaked bread slices.
4. Using an electric mixer on low setting combine bread and egg, mixing for about 15 seconds.
5. Add onion and garlic to bread mixture, and beat for another 10 seconds to mix thoroughly.

6. Select a large skillet with an airtight cover. Coat cooking surface with olive oil.
7. Rinse veal cutlets and lay them out on a sheet of waxed paper.
8. Divide bread mixture evenly among veal cutlets, placing about a tablespoon in the center of each cutlet.
9. Roll cutlet around bread mixture, and secure each with a toothpick, forming a "veal bird."
10. Preheat prepared skillet over medium heat and gently add the veal birds.
11. Brown veal birds for about 5 minutes.
12. Turn veal birds over gently, and brown the other side, for about 5 minutes.
13. Remove mushroom soup from can to a small mixing bowl; add 1/4 cup milk. Whisk until smooth.
14. Pour mushroom soup mixture over veal birds. Cover skillet and place in oven.
15. Bake for about an hour, checking after about three quarters of an hour. If it becomes dry, add another ¼ cup of milk, and stir gently. Replace cover and return birds to oven for remaining 15 minutes.
16. Remove veal birds from oven and distribute evenly among 6 serving plates. Spoon mushroom gravy evenly over the 6 portions.

PRESTO! PESTO SAUCED FLOUNDER

YIELD: Serves 4

Per portion:

GI: 30
GL: 1.7

CALORIES: 253.5; Carbohydrates: 5.5g; Fiber: .63g; Protein: 25g; Fat: 21.62g; Saturated Fats: 2.87g; Sodium: 135.88mg

INGREDIENTS:

- 1 pound flounder fillets
- 1 tbsp. extra virgin olive oil
- 1/2 cup packed fresh basil leaves
- 1/2 cup packed fresh parsley
- 3 tbsp. pine nuts
- 1/4 cup freshly grated parmesan cheese
- 2 tbsp. minced fresh garlic
- 2 tbsp. fresh cilantro leaves
- 2 tbsp. lemon juice
- 2 tbsp. chopped shallots
- 3 tbsp. extra virgin olive oil

PREPARATION:

1. Preheat oven to 400 degrees.
2. Coat cooking surface of large skillet (select one with an airtight cover) with 1 tbsp. olive oil.
3. Arrange flounder fillets in skillet.
4. Combine remaining 9 ingredients in food processor or blender. Process until smooth, scraping sides as needed, creating pesto.
5. Spread Pesto over fillets.

6. Cover skillet and cook flounder in oven for about 20 minutes, until it flakes easily with a fork.
7. Distribute fillets evenly to 4 serving plates and spoon 1/4 of pesto sauce over the top of each.

SNAPPY BAKED LUMP CRAB CAKES

YIELD: Serves 3

Per portion:

GI: 55
GL: 4.58

CALORIES: 162.55; Carbohydrates: 8.33g; Fiber: 1.67g; Protein: 14g; Fat: 8.5g; Saturated Fats: 3.3g; Sodium: 266.08mg

INGREDIENTS:

- 8 ounces canned lump crab meat, drained
- 1 slice Healthy Choice 7 Grain bread (Con Agra, USA), dried and grated
- 1 tsp. crab boil seasoning
- 1 tsp. finely chopped fresh parsley
- 1 tbsp. mayonnaise
- 1 tbsp. butter, melted
- 1 extra-large egg, well beaten
- 1 tsp. Worcestershire sauce
- 1 tsp. mustard powder
- 1 green onion, finely shopped
- 1 tsp. minced garlic
- 1 tbsp. freshly squeezed lemon juice
- Canola oil cooking spray

PREPARATION:

1. Preheat oven to 375 degrees.
2. Coat cooking surface of baking dish with 1/3 second spray of canola oil cooking spray.

3. In a medium sized mixing bowl, combine lemon juice, crab boil seasoning, egg, Worcestershire sauce, mayonnaise, and melted butter. Whisk well to combine ingredients.
4. In a small mixing bowl, combine bread crumbs, mustard powder, minced garlic, parsley, and green onion.
5. Add crab meat to egg mixture, mixing carefully to gently coat crab meat.
6. Finally, add breadcrumb mixture to egg-coated crab mixture, stirring gently to coat crab with crumb mixture.
7. Form into 3 three quarter inch thick patties, and place on baking dish in oven for 6 minutes.
8. Turn patties over, and bake for another 6 to 10 minutes until they brown slightly and form crispy edges...
9. Place one crab cake on each of 3 serving plates.

DINNERS TO LOVE

ENTREES

ALBERTO'S TEXAS STYLE CHILI

YIELD: Serves 4

Per portion:

GI: 50
GL: 8.98

CALORIES: 238.13; Carbohydrates: 17.96g; Fiber: 4.9g; Protein: 24.75g; Fat: 4.28g; Saturated Fats: 4g; Sodium: 115mg.

INGREDIENTS:

- 1 lb. hamburger, 95% lean
- 1/2 cup chopped onion
- 1/2 cup chopped tomatoes
- 1 cup of water
- 1 cup kidney beans, soaked, cooked without salt, and their liquid
- 1/2 tsp. horseradish
- 1 tbsp. chili powder
- 1 tbsp. oregano
- 1 tsp. cumin powder
- 1 tbsp. minced fresh garlic
- 1/4 tsp. freshly ground black peppercorns, to taste
- 1 tsp. cayenne pepper

PREPARATION:

1. Place the tomatoes and 1 cup of water in a large stainless steel Dutch oven. Add kidney beans, horseradish, and spices.
2. Cover and simmer over medium heat for 1 hour and 15 minutes. Add small amounts of water as needed if the mixture thickens too much.
3. While the beans simmer, cook hamburger, garlic and onions, in a skillet. Drain excess fat and blot with a paper towel to remove remaining fat.

4. Add hamburger mixture to the simmering kidney bean mixture. Stir to combine, and then replace cover.
5. Reduce heat to low. Simmer together for another 15 minutes, stirring occasionally.
6. Ladle chili equally into 4 serving bowls.

BAKED CHICKEN PARMESAN

YIELD: Serves 4

Per portion:

GI: 50
GL: 4.19

CALORIES: 297.28; Carbohydrates: 8.38g; Fiber: 1.38g; Protein: 34.5g; Fat: 19.75g; Saturated Fats: 4.75g; Sodium: 461.75mg

INGREDIENTS:

- Four 4 oz. fresh skinless and boneless chicken breasts
- 1 cup no salt added tomato sauce
- 1 cup freshly grated Parmesan cheese
- 1/2 cup chopped onion
- 1 tbsp. minced fresh garlic
- 1/8 tsp. freshly ground black peppercorns, to taste
- 1 tbsp. extra virgin olive oil

PREPARATION:

1. Preheat oven to 350 degrees.
2. Season chicken breasts with freshly ground black peppercorns.
3. Place chicken breasts on a skillet coated with olive oil.
4. Arrange chopped onion and garlic over chicken breasts.
5. Cover skillet with an airtight lid, and bake in oven for about 40 minutes and chicken is tender. (You may want to add a bit of water if the lid is not air tight so the chicken stays moist.)
6. Top chicken with tomato sauce and sprinkle with grated Parmesan cheese.
7. Bake another five minutes uncovered, until tomato sauce is bubbly hot, and parmesan cheese melts.
8. Distribute chicken and sauce evenly onto 4 serving plates.

BAKED TILAPIA MARINATED IN
ITALIAN DRESSING

YIELD: Serves 4

Per portion:

GI: <1
GL: <1

CALORIES: 151.06; Carbohydrates: 2.63g; Fiber: .31g; Protein: 24.13g; Fat: 3.5g; Saturated Fats: .25g; Sodium: 225.75mg

INGREDIENTS:

- 4 tilapia filets, 4 oz. each
- 1/4 cup fat-free Italian dressing (approx. 2 tbsp. per filet)
- 2 tbsp. snipped fresh chives
- 2 tbsp. chopped fresh shallots
- 9 sprigs fresh cilantro
- 1 tbsp. extra virgin olive oil

PREPARATION:

1. Preheat oven to 375 degrees.
2. In a medium sized bowl, marinate four tilapia filets in 1/2 cup fat-free Italian dressing and chopped chives for 30 minutes.
3. Place tilapia filets on glass baking dish coated with olive oil.
4. Bake tilapia filets and marinade together at 375 degrees for ten to twelve minutes or until fish flakes easily with a fork. You may want to add a bit of water to keep tilapia moist.
5. Distribute tilapia and sauce evenly among 4 serving plates.
6. Garnish with fresh sprigs of cilantro.

BLACK BEAN VEGGIE SOUP

YIELD: Serves 4

Per portion:

GI: 40
GL: 9.62

CALORIES: 270; Carbohydrates: 24.06g; Fiber: 9.32g; Protein: 15.56g; Fat: 2g; Saturated Fats: 1g; Sodium: 39.5mg

INGREDIENTS:

- 2 cups black beans, cooked without salt, drained
- 2 cups organic low sodium vegetable broth
- 1/4 cup chopped green pepper
- 1/2 cup diced celery
- 1/4 cup chopped onion
- 1 tbsp. minced fresh garlic
- 1/2 tsp. freshly ground black pepper
- 1 tsp. chopped fresh cilantro
- 2 tsp. chopped fresh parsley
- 4 tbsp. sour cream
- Canola oil cooking spray

PREPARATION:

1. Bring black beans and vegetable broth to a boil in large, covered Dutch oven.
2. Lightly spray a large skillet with a 1/3 second spray of canola oil cooking spray. Place skillet over medium heat.
3. Add green pepper, onion and celery to skillet. Cook stirring occasionally for about 3 minutes, until vegetables become tender and onion becomes translucent.
4. Add garlic to vegetables in skillet and cook for just a minute until garlic releases its aroma.

5. Add sautéed vegetables, cilantro, and parsley to black bean and broth mixture. Bring to a boil, cover, lower heat, and simmer for about 45 minutes, stirring occasionally and mashing some of the beans with your spoon each time you stir. You may add water to prevent scorching and achieve the consistency you desire.
6. Ladle equally into 4 serving bowls.
7. Garnish each serving with 1 tbsp. of sour cream.

CAROLINA'S CURRIED MEATLOAF

YIELD: Serves 4

Per portion:

GI: 40
GL: 3.37

CALORIES: 266; Carbohydrates: 8.42g; Fiber: 2.63g; Protein: 29.41g; Fat: 10.5g; Saturated Fats: 5g; Sodium: 196.63mg

INGREDIENTS:

- 1 lb. 95% lean ground beef
- 1 c. fresh small apples, chopped coarsely
- 1/4 cup chopped fresh purple onion
- 1/4 cup chopped fresh red bell pepper
- 2 1/2 tsp. curry powder
- 1 tsp. minced fresh garlic
- 2 extra-large eggs
- 1 oz. almond meal

PREPARATION:

1. Preheat oven to 350 degrees.
2. Combine eggs, garlic, 2 tsp. curry powder, and almond meal. Whisk until slightly fluffy.
3. In a large bowl, combine apple, purple onion, red pepper and ground beef; mixing well.
4. Pour egg mixture over ground beef mixture combining ingredients thoroughly.
5. Shape into a loaf and place in 9 X 5 inch glass loaf pan.
6. Sprinkle with salt, pepper, and remaining 1/2 tsp. curry powder.
7. Bake for 1 hour, uncovered.
8. Slice meatloaf into 4 equal servings.

SLOW SAUTE' CHICKEN WITH VEGETABLES

YIELD: Serves 4

Per portion:

GI: 40
GL: 4.57

CALORIES: 283.75; Carbohydrates: 11.43g; Fiber: 7.75g; Protein: 26.3g; Fat: 12.56g; Saturated Fats: 1.5g; Sodium: 100.75mg

INGREDIENTS:

- four 4 oz. fresh skinless, boneless chicken breasts
- 1 cup chopped sweet onion
- 1 cup chopped celery
- 1 cup broccoli florets
- 3 tbsp. extra virgin olive oil
- 2 tbsp. flax seeds
- 3 tbsp. cinnamon

PREPARATION:

1. Heat 3 tbsp. olive oil in stainless steel Dutch oven over medium heat on stove top, being sure to coat all cooking surfaces with oil.
2. Rinse and place skinless chicken breasts in Dutch oven. Sprinkle with 1/2 of the flax seeds.
3. Cover and cook for 8 minutes; uncover, turn chicken over and sprinkle with remaining flax seeds.
4. Add the onion, celery and broccoli florets to chicken mixture.
5. Reduce heat to low and cook for an additional 20 minutes, adding water if necessary so chicken and vegetables do not stick.
6. Sprinkle the cinnamon on the chicken and vegetable mixture. Stir well.
7. Cover and cook chicken breasts until they easily break into pieces.

8. Simmer gently over very low heat for an additional 10 minutes.
9. Place chicken breasts equally onto 4 serving plates, and top each serving with ¼ of vegetables.

DILLY WHITE SEA BASS

YIELD: Serves 4

Per portion:

GI: 40
GL: 3

CALORIES: 228.5; Carbohydrate: 7.5g; Fiber: 2.33; Protein: 33g; Fat: 7.75g; Saturated Fats: .5g; Sodium: 195mg

INGREDIENTS:

- 4 filets White Sea bass, approximately 4 oz. each
- 1/2 cup chopped white onion
- 2 tbsp. capers
- 1 tsp. finely ground mustard seed
- 1 tbsp. extra virgin olive oil
- 2 oz. freshly squeezed lemon juice
- 2 tbsp. fresh chopped dill
- 2 tbsp. pine nuts
- 1 tbsp. minced garlic
- 1 tbsp. dried dill weed
- 4 sprigs fresh dill

PREPARATION:

1. Preheat oven to 400 degrees.
2. Mix onion, capers, mustard, dried dill weed, pine nuts, garlic, lemon juice, and fresh chopped dill in a small bowl.
3. Coat cooking surface of glass baking dish with olive oil, and arrange White Sea bass over cooking surface.
4. Spoon freshly squeezed lemon juice evenly over fish fillets.
5. Spread the onion-dill mixture evenly over the White Sea bass fillets.

6. Bake in oven for about 10 minutes until opaque throughout, and the fish flakes easily with a fork.
7. Distribute White Sea Bass among 4 serving plates and top each serving with 1/4 of the onion-dill sauce remaining in the baking dish.
8. Garnish each serving with a sprig of fresh dill.

FRESH COD FILLETS

YIELD: Serves 4

Per portion:

GI: 40
GL: 3.15

CALORIES: 235.38; Carbohydrates: 7.87g; Fiber: 1.25g; Protein: 30.5g; Fat: 9g; Saturated Fats: 1g; Sodium: 162.75mg

INGREDIENTS:

- 4 fresh cod filets, 6-oz. each
- 1/2 cup red grapefruit
- 1 cup chopped sweet purple onion
- 2 tbsp. extra virgin olive oil
- 1 oz. chopped fresh cilantro
- 1 tsp. paprika
- 1 tbsp. capers, drained
- 1 tbsp. chopped, fresh marjoram

PREPARATION:

1. Preheat oven to 400 degrees.
2. Coat glass baking dish with 1 tbsp. olive oil. Place cod filets in baking dish.
3. Chop grapefruit, pulp included, into fine pieces and place in mixing bowl.
4. Add chopped onion, remaining tablespoon of olive oil, cilantro, capers, and marjoram. Mix well.
5. Pour this mixture over the cod filets; turning fillets to cover both sides.
6. Sprinkle with paprika.
7. Bake for approximately 10 minutes, until cod flakes easily with a fork.
8. Divide cod fillets equally onto 4 serving plates and spoon remaining baked marinade equally over the 4 servings of fish.

GREEK SCAMPI SHRIMP

YIELD: Serves 4

Per portion:

GI: 40
GL: 4.25

CALORIES: 324.42; Carbohydrates: 10.63g; Fiber: 2g; Protein: 38.25g; Fat: 10.5g; Saturated Fats: .75g; Sodium: 278.98mg

INGREDIENTS:

- 1 1/2 lbs. of fresh large shrimp
- 1 cup sliced fresh mushrooms
- 1/4 cup minced garlic
- 1 cup fresh sweet red bell peppers
- 2 fresh green onion stalks, sliced into rings
- 1/4 cup fresh chopped parsley
- 1/4 cup balsamic vinegar
- 3 tbsp. extra virgin olive oil
- 1 tsp. Worcestershire sauce
- 1/2 tsp. Tabasco sauce
- 1 tsp. chopped fresh parsley
- 1/8 tsp. cayenne pepper, to taste

PREPARATION:

1. Rinse, peel and devein the fresh shrimp; set aside covered in refrigerator.
2. Rinse the red peppers; remove seeds and chop coarsely.
3. Rinse and dry the mushrooms and slice.
4. Heat 2 tbsp. of olive oil in large sauté skillet over medium heat, being sure to cover the cooking surface.

5. Add the shrimp and cook quickly, moving them around in the pan; raise heat if necessary to slightly sear the shrimp, and slightly brown the exteriors. Move them to the outer sides of the skillet.
6. Add the remaining tbsp. olive oil and then the red peppers and garlic to the middle of the skillet; cook, stirring frequently for about two minutes.
7. Pour in the vinegar and then add the mushrooms to the middle of the skillet. Sprinkle with cayenne pepper.
8. Stir all together, and cover while cooking for about 3 minutes, stirring occasionally.
9. Remove from heat; add chopped parsley; stir lightly and cover skillet. Allow to stand for just a minute before serving.
10. Distribute shrimp and vegetables equally among 4 serving plates.

GRILLED SWORDFISH IN WHITE WINE AND LEMON SAUCE

YIELD: Serves 2

Per portion:

GI: <1
GL: <1

CALORIES: 229.91; Carbohydrate: 6.26g; Fiber: .75; Protein: 32.5g; Fat: 2.5g; Saturated Fats: 0g; Sodium: 443mg

INGREDIENTS:

- 2 swordfish steaks, 5 ounces each
- 1/4 cup white cooking wine
- 2 oz. freshly squeezed lemon juice
- 1 tsp. Tamari® Soy sauce
- 2 tsp. Worcestershire sauce
- 2 tbsp. freshly minced garlic
- 1/2 tsp. chopped fresh rosemary
- 1 tsp. of freshly ground black peppercorns, to taste
- 1 tsp. chopped fresh thyme
- 1 tbsp. chopped fresh chives

PREPARATION:

1. Preheat oven or barbeque grill to 400 degrees.
2. Rinse the swordfish steaks with cool water, pat dry, and set aside.
3. For marinade, combine next 7 ingredients in a medium bowl.
4. Place the swordfish in the marinade, cover. Let stand for a few hours or overnight in the refrigerator.
5. Cook the swordfish on a baking rack in the oven or on the grill for about 10 minutes or until fish flakes easily with a fork.

6. While the swordfish is cooking, pour the remaining marinade into a small saucepan and place over medium heat. Cook, stirring constantly until mixture comes to a boil.
7. Remove swordfish from cooking surface to two serving plates. Spoon half of sauce over each swordfish fillet.
8. Garnish with chopped fresh thyme and chives.

FILLET OF SOLE IN MUSTARD SAUCE

YIELD: Serves 4

Per portion:

GI: 40
GL: 2

CALORIES: 196.65; Carbohydrates: 5g; Fiber: .75g; Protein: 25.5g; Fat: 4g; Saturated Fats: 0g; Sodium: 487.35mg

INGREDIENTS:

- 4 Sole Fillets, 5 ounces each
- 1 cup sliced mushrooms
- 1/2 cup sliced onion
- 1/4 cup very finely chopped red bell
- 1 tbsp. chopped shallots
- 1 tbsp. minced fresh garlic
- 1 tbsp. plus 1 tsp. mayonnaise
- 2 tbsp. Dijon mustard
- 2 tbsp. extra virgin olive oil

PREPARATION:

1. Preheat oven to 400 degrees.
2. Cover cooking surface of a small saucepan with 1 tbsp. olive oil.
3. Add onion, garlic, shallots, and red bell pepper to sauce pan and cook over medium heat for about 2 minutes, or until vegetables are tender. Remove from heat, cover, and set aside to cool for about 10 minutes.
4. Cover cooking surface of glass baking dish with 1 tbsp. olive oil.
5. Arrange sole on glass baking dish.
6. In a small mixing bowl, combine mustard and mayonnaise well.
7. Add vegetables to mayonnaise mixture. Combine the two mixtures into one to form a thick sauce.

8. Spread sauce on top of sole fillets.
9. Bake fish for about 10 minutes, until mustard sauce is bubbling and browned, and sole flakes easily with a fork.
10. Distribute sole and sauce equally among 4 serving plates.
11. Garnish each serving with a fresh parsley sprig.

HERBED FISH WEDGES WITH COLESLAW

YIELD: Serves 4

Per portion:

GI: 40
GL: 4.64

CALORIES: 253.75; Carbohydrates: 11.6g; Fiber: 3.63; Protein: 27.5g; Fat: 11.38g; Saturated Fat: .25g; Sodium: 135.13mg

INGREDIENTS: *Fish*

- 4 whitefish filets (about 5 oz. each)
- 2 tsp. chopped, fresh dill
- 2 tbsp. finely grated lemon rind
- 1/2 tsp. cayenne
- 1/2 tsp. paprika
- 1/2 tsp. garlic powder
- 1/2 tsp. chili powder
- 1/2 tsp. finely ground mustard seed
- 1/2 tsp. dried basil
- 1/2 tsp. freshly ground black peppercorns, to taste

INGREDIENTS: *Coleslaw*

- 3 cups cabbage, finely shredded
- 1/2 cup shredded carrot
- 1/2 red onion, finely chopped
- 1/4 cup chopped fresh parsley
- 1 tbsp. low-sodium, reduced-calorie mayonnaise
- 1 oz. freshly squeezed lemon juice

PREPARATION: *Fish*

1. Preheat the oven to 400 degrees and line a large baking tray with parchment paper.
2. Meanwhile, tear four 12 inch squares of parchment paper.
3. In a small mixing bowl, combine cayenne, paprika, garlic powder, chili powder, basil, and finely ground mustard seed.
4. Place a whitefish filet on each of 4 sheets of parchment paper and sprinkle seasoning mixture over each whitefish filet. Top each with dusting of fresh dill and grated lemon rind. Season to taste with freshly ground black peppercorns.
5. Fold and wrap the parchment paper securely to enclose the whitefish and place on a baking dish. Bake for 12 minutes or until whitefish flakes easily with a fork.

PREPARATION: *Coleslaw*

1. Combine the cabbage, carrot, onion, and parsley in a large bowl.
2. Add the mayonnaise and lemon juice; toss to combine.
3. Serve 1/4 of the coleslaw with each of the 4 whitefish wedges.

EASY CHEESY TURKEY BURGERS

YIELD: Serves 6

Per portion:

GI: 40
GL: 1.2

CALORIES: 240.66; Carbohydrates: 3g; Fiber: .67g; Protein: 25.08g; Fat: 13.58g; Saturated Fats: 3.67g; Sodium: 223.5mg

INGREDIENTS:

- 1 ½ lbs. lean ground turkey
- 1 cup fresh mushrooms, sliced
- 1 cup Kraft® reduced-fat cheddar cheese, shredded
- 1 tbsp. flaxseeds
- 2 oz. finely minced onion
- 1 tbsp. minced garlic
- 1 tbsp. extra virgin olive oil
- 1/8 tsp. freshly ground black peppercorns, to taste

PREPARATION:

1. In a large mixing bowl, combine onion and garlic, then add the cheese, stirring to combine. Add ground turkey and mix well.
2. Coat cooking surface of large skillet with olive oil.
3. Heat skillet over medium low heat.
4. Add 1 tbsp. flaxseeds to the pan, then mushrooms. Cover and cook for 2-3 minutes. Remove mushroom mixture to warm plate, cover, and set aside.
5. Add turkey patties to skillet; cover and cook for 3-4 minutes or until thoroughly done, turning once after about 2 minutes.
6. Distribute burgers to 6 serving plates.
7. Garnish each burger with a sixth of the mushroom mixture.

CHICKEN STROGANOFF

YIELD: Serves 4

Per portion:

GI: 40
GL: 3.23

CALORIES: 305; Carbohydrates: 8.07g; Fiber: .93g; Protein: 30g; Fat: 7.67g; Saturated Fats: 4.87g; Sodium: 252mg

INGREDIENTS:

- 1 lb. diced chicken breast
- 2 cups sliced mushrooms
- 1 cup diced onion
- 1 cup light sour cream
- 1/2 cup low sodium chicken broth
- 1/2 cup 1% low-fat milk
- 1 tbsp. prepared Dijon mustard
- 1/2 tsp. freshly ground black peppercorns, to taste
- 1 tbsp. almond meal flour
- 1 tbsp. extra virgin olive oil

PREPARATION:

1. Coat the cooking surface of a large skillet with olive oil, and preheat over medium heat.
2. Add the onions and mushrooms, cover, and cook until tender or to taste. Remove vegetables from skillet to a warm plate and cover.
3. Add the diced chicken breast to the skillet, cover and cook for about 10 minutes, stirring occasionally.
4. While the chicken is cooking, pour chicken broth in a small glass, and add the flour, pepper, and Dijon mustard, whisking well with a fork, until mixture is combined and free of lumps.

5. Add the vegetables, milk, and sour cream to the skillet; cook over medium heat until mixture begins to boil, stirring frequently.
6. Pour in the broth mixture, and stir constantly until mixture returns to boiling. You may continue to cook mixture, uncovered, until it is the thickness you prefer.
7. Distribute Chicken Stroganoff mixture evenly among 4 serving plates.

ORANGE AND FENNEL SEA SCALLOPS

YIELD: Serves 4

Per portion:

GI: 40
GL: 4.4

CALORIES: 165.5; Carbohydrates: 11g; Fiber: 1.25g; Protein: 20.75g; Fat: 3.75g; Saturated Fats: .5g; Sodium: 185.25mg

INGREDIENTS:

- 1 lb. of large sea scallops
- 2 tbsp. extra virgin olive oil
- 1 tbsp. crushed fennel seeds
- 2 tbsp. minced garlic
- 2 tbsp. freshly grated orange rind
- 1 cup 1 inch fresh zucchini cubes
- 1 cup sweet red onion wedges
- 2 tbsp. chopped fresh parsley
- 4 skewers, soaked in water for 20 minutes

PREPARATION:

1. Rinse, dry gently and chop parsley; crush the fennel seeds; grate the orange rind.
2. Put these 3 ingredients in a mixing bowl; add the olive oil and minced garlic; then whisk all together vigorously for a few seconds.
3. Add the scallops and cover. Marinade for a couple of hours or overnight in refrigerator.
4. Onto 4 skewers, thread the onion, zucchini and scallops. Begin with a slice of zucchini; add a piece of onion, then a scallop. Repeat until all 4 skewers are evenly full.

5. Preheat broiler for 5 minutes. Place the skewers on a broiler pan under broiler for about 5 minutes. Turn and continue broiling for another 5 minutes or until scallops are cooked thoroughly. Broil a bit longer if you like them a bit crispy.
6. Sprinkle with fresh chopped parsley.
7. Distribute onto 4 serving plates and serve immediately.

PORK TENDERLOIN WITH
GINGER-APPLE GLAZE

YIELD: Serves 4

Per portion:

GI: 39
GL: 2.73

CALORIES: 163.25; Carbohydrates: 7g; Fiber: .5g; Protein: 24g; Fat: 4g; Saturated Fats: 0g; Sodium: 60mg

INGREDIENTS:

- 16 oz. lean pork tenderloin, sliced into 1/2 inch rounds
- 2 cups peeled golden delicious apple slices
- 1 tsp. apple cider vinegar
- 1 tbsp. minced fresh ginger
- 1 – 2 drops liquid stevia
- 1/2 cup water

PREPARATION:

1. Preheat oven to 350 degrees.
2. Sear pork tenderloin rounds in a large, heavy skillet over medium heat on stove top, stirring occasionally, until gently browned on all sides, for about 20 minutes.
3. Place browned tenderloins in baking dish with 1/2 cup water. Cover.
4. Bake at 350 degrees for 20 minutes.
5. Place apples in a small skillet. Add 1/2 c. water, ginger, stevia, and apple cider vinegar. Cover.
6. Cook apple mixture for about 10 minutes over low medium heat or until apples become tender to taste and sauce begins to boil and thicken slightly.

7. Remove pork tenderloin from oven, distributing evenly among 4 warm serving plates.
8. Spoon 1/4 of Ginger-Apple Glaze equally over each of the four tenderloin round servings.

PORTOBELLO LAMB KA-BOBS

YIELD: Serves 4

Per portion:

GI: 40
GL: 3.2

CALORIES: 375.25; Carbohydrates: 8g; Fiber: .25g; Protein: 20.75g; Fat: 21.95g; Saturated Fats: 10.25g; Sodium: 82.75mg

INGREDIENTS:

- 1 lb. lean lamb
- 1 tbsp. minced fresh garlic
- 1 cup sliced Portobello mushroom tops
- 1 cup cubed whole fresh sweet red bell pepper, seeds removed
- 1 cup fresh sweet purple onion wedges
- 2 tbsp. pure sesame oil
- 3 tbsp. apple cider vinegar
- 4 skewers, soaked in water for 20 minutes

PREPARATION:

1. Cube lamb into 1-inch pieces and place in large bowl.
2. Place vegetables in bowl with lamb cuts.
3. Combine apple cider vinegar, garlic, and sesame oil in a small bowl.
4. Pour oil and vinegar mixture over lamb and vegetable mixture, stirring gently to coat all pieces. Cover and let marinade for at least 1 hour in the refrigerator.
5. Preheat oven to 375 degrees.
6. Thread mushroom, pepper, onion and then lamb pieces onto skewers; continue to alternate in this pattern until all 4 skewers are equal servings.
7. Place skewers onto large glass baking dish.
8. Baste with remaining marinade.
9. Bake for 35 minutes, until lamb is tender.

SIDE DISH: KA-BOB BEDS

YIELD: Serves 4

Per portion:

GI: 39
GL: 6.72

CALORIES: 101; Carbohydrates: 17.25g; Fiber: 9.25g; Protein: 7g; Fat: 0g; Saturated Fats: 0g; Sodium: 2.25mg

INGREDIENTS:

- 1/2 cup green lentils, dried
- 1 tsp. curry powder
- 1/2 tsp. chopped fresh basil
- 1 cup water

PREPARATION:

1. Rinse and sort lentils in a small stainless steel Dutch oven.
2. Cover with 1 cup water.
3. Bring to boil over medium-high heat in covered stainless steel Dutch oven.
4. Add curry powder and fresh basil.
5. Reduce heat, and simmer for about 45 minutes, until lentils are tender and water is absorbed.
6. Place one fourth of lentil mixture on each serving plate.
7. Top with a serving of tender Lamb Ka-Bob.
8. Serve immediately.

RAINBOW TROUT WITH BROCCOLI

YIELD: Serves 4

Per portion:

GI: 40
GL: 6.75

CALORIES: 331.88; Carbohydrates: 16.88g; Fiber: 5.75g; Protein: 38.25g; Fat: 13g; Saturated Fats: .5g; Sodium: 368.13mg

INGREDIENTS:

- 4 filets rainbow trout, about 6 ounces each
- 1 cup sliced mushrooms
- 1 1/2 cups fresh or frozen broccoli flowerets
- 1/4 cup celery sliced in 1/2 inch thick pieces
- 1/2 cup carrots, sliced diagonally into 1/2 inch thickness
- 1/3 cup chopped green onions and tops
- 1/2 cup dry white cooking wine
- 3/4 cup clam juice
- 1 fresh lemon, sliced into 4 segments
- 1 tbsp. freshly squeezed lemon juice
- 1 tbsp. freshly minced garlic
- 1/2 tsp. crushed oregano leaves
- 1/2 tsp. crushed thyme
- 4 sprigs fresh parsley
- 1/2 tsp. freshly ground black peppercorns, to taste
- 2 tbsp. extra virgin olive oil

PREPARATION:

1. Coat cooking surface of shallow baking dish with 1 tbsp. olive oil.
2. Rinse trout thoroughly and place in oil coated baking dish.

3. Combine clam juice, wine, lemon juice, oregano, thyme and black pepper in a small bowl. Pour mixture over trout. Cover and refrigerate for 3-4 hours.
4. Drain trout, reserving marinade.
5. In a wok or large skillet, sauté broccoli, celery, mushrooms, carrot, green onion slices, and garlic in 1 tbsp. olive oil over medium heat for about 5 minutes, until just crisp-tender or to taste. Push vegetables to outer sides of wok.
6. Raise heat to medium-high. Add trout, cooking for 2-3 minutes on each side, until lightly browned.
7. Add reserved marinade; cover wok, simmer until fish flakes easily with a fork, for about 5 minutes.
8. Transfer trout and vegetables equally to four serving plates.
9. Boil reserved marinade mixture until reduced to about 1/3 cup, for about 3 minutes.
10. Pour 1/4 of reduced marinade mixture equally over each of the 4 servings of fish. Garnish each serving with a lemon segment and sprig of fresh parsley.

SHRIMP STUFFED FLOUNDER ROLL-UPS

YIELD: Serves 4

Per portion:

GI: 55
GL: 7.29

CALORIES: 302.75; Carbohydrates: 13.25g; Fiber: 1g; Protein: 36.75g; Fat: 7.75g; Saturated Fats: 1g; Sodium: 349mg

INGREDIENTS:

- 4 four oz. flounder fillets, rinsed and patted dry
- 1/2 pound peeled and deveined shrimp, chopped
- 3 slices Healthy Choice 7 Grain bread, dried and grated
- 1/2 cup thinly sliced celery
- 1/2 cup finely chopped onion
- 1 tbsp. minced garlic
- 2 tbsp. extra virgin olive oil
- 2 tbsp. freshly grated parmesan cheese
- 1/4 cup white cooking wine
- 1 tbsp. finely chopped fresh parsley

PREPARATION:

1. Preheat oven to 375 degrees.
2. Heat 1 tbsp. of the oil in a medium sized skillet over medium heat.
3. Add the shrimp, garlic, onion, and celery, and cook, stirring frequently for about 4 minutes, or until the shrimp is opaque. Remove from heat.
4. In a medium sized mixing bowl, combine the bread crumbs and parmesan cheese.
5. Add the shrimp mixture to the bread crumb mixture, and combine well to form stuffing mixture.
6. Place flounder fillets on waxed paper.

7. Evenly divide the stuffing mixture among the four flounder fillets, spreading to within 1/2 inch of the edges.
8. Roll the flounder fillets beginning with the thin end to encase the stuffing.
9. Secure each Roll-Up with a wooden toothpick.
10. Spread remaining 1 tbsp. olive oil over cooking surface of 6 X 8 inch glass baking dish.
11. Arrange the Flounder Roll-ups in the glass baking dish.
12. Pour the cooking wine over the Flounder Roll-ups. Sprinkle with chopped parsley.
13. Bake in 375 degree oven for 12-16 minutes or until flounder flakes easily with a fork.
14. Distribute flounder and juices equally among 4 warm serving plates.

SPICY BAKED CHICKEN AND VEGETABLES IN A FOIL PACK

YIELD: Serves 2

Per portion:

GI: 40
GL: 7.40

CALORIES: 209; Carbohydrates: 18.5g; Fiber: 4.5g; Protein: 26.6g; Fat: 0g; Saturated Fats: g; Sodium: 100.5mg

INGREDIENTS:

- 2 four oz. skinless, boneless chicken breast
- 1 cup sliced fresh fennel bulb
- 8 oz. fresh snap green beans
- 1/2 cup sliced white sweet Spanish onion
- 1 tbsp. cardamom
- 1 oz. red hot chili pepper, sliced, deseeded and chopped (Do not touch with your bare hands.)
- 1 tsp. Mrs. Dash® Southwest Chipotle Seasoning
- 1 tbsp. minced fresh garlic
- 2 tbsp. red cooking wine
- 1 oz. fresh lemon juice

PREPARATION:

1. Preheat oven to 350 degrees.
2. Make 2 aluminum foil packets twice as large as necessary to enclose one half of chicken and vegetables. Fold each foil piece in half to thicken it.
3. Place one half of fennel, onion, and green beans in the middle of each foil piece.
4. Sprinkle each with half of cardamom.

5. Place one chicken breast on top of each pile of vegetables, and sprinkle with 1/2 tsp. Mrs. Dash® Seasoning.
6. Mix the chili, garlic, pepper, wine, and lemon juice together in a small cup. Spoon an equal amount over each chicken breast.
7. Fold foil over chicken and vegetables, turning the edges together tightly to close pack so as not to allow steam to escape. Place foil packets on a tray in the oven for 45-60 minutes.
8. Remove foil packets to serving plates. Serve chicken in foil packets on plates. Open slowly, allowing steam to escape.

STEAK WITH ARTICHOKE HEARTS IN RED WINE SAUCE

YIELD: Serves 2

Per portion:

GI: 40
GL: 6.26

CALORIES: 407.75; Carbohydrates: 15.65g; Fiber: 5g; Protein: 33.1g; Fat: 23.5g; Saturated Fats: 6.7g; Sodium: 369.75mg

INGREDIENTS:

- 11 oz. chuck steak, trimmed of visible fat, and cut into 2 equal pieces
- One 10 oz. package frozen artichoke hearts, thawed
- 1/2 cup Campbell's® Fat-free Beef Gravy
- 1 tbsp. extra virgin olive oil
- 1/2 cup chopped fresh onion
- 3 tbsp. red cooking wine
- 1 tsp. minced fresh garlic

PREPARATION:

1. Coat the surface of a baking dish with olive oil. Place the steak on the dish; pour the red wine and garlic on top and set aside for 15-20 minutes.
2. While steak is marinating, preheat the oven to 375 degrees for 10 minutes.
3. Add artichoke hearts and onion to steak and wine mixture.
4. Cover the baking dish tightly and bake steaks for 20 minutes. Then turn the steaks over, reduce the heat to 325 degrees and bake for an additional 20 minutes.
5. Prepare the gravy according package directions.
6. Remove steak to 2 warm serving plates.
7. Place half of vegetable mixture around each steak. Top each serving with 1/4 cup gravy.

STRIPED BASS WITH SOUR CREAM AND CHEESE

YIELD: Serves 3

Per portion:

GI: 50
GL: 3.50

CALORIES: 292.17; Carbohydrates: 7g; Fiber: 1g; Protein: 33.3g; Fat: 14.67g; Saturated Fats: 5.67g; Sodium: 373mg

INGREDIENTS:

- 3 four oz. striped bass filets
- 1 cup shredded low-fat cheddar cheese
- 3/4 cup low-fat sour cream
- 1 tsp. paprika
- 2 tsp. chili powder
- 1/2 tsp. dried oregano
- 1/2 cup chopped tomato
- 1 tsp. Tabasco® Sauce
- 1 oz. freshly squeezed lemon juice

PREPARATION:

1. Preheat oven to 400 degrees.
2. Drizzle lemon over fish filets.
3. Combine sour cream, chili powder, oregano, tomato, Tabasco® Sauce, and paprika in a medium- size bowl. Mix well.
4. Dip filets in sour cream mixture, coating both sides. Place in a glass casserole dish.
5. Sprinkle cheese equally on the tops of the fish filets.

6. Bake in oven approximately 10 minutes or until fish flakes easily with a fork.
7. Distribute bass evenly among 3 warm serving plates.

TERIYAKI FLANK STEAK

YIELD: Serves 8

Per portion:

GI: 40
GL: 3.7

CALORIES: 308.13; Carbohydrates: 9.25g; Fiber: 1.63g; Protein: 36g; Fat: 14.13g; Saturated Fats: 4.25g; Sodium: 800.75mg

INGREDIENTS:

- 2 lbs. flank steak with all fat trimmed
- 3 cups sliced mushrooms
- 1/2 cup minced onion
- 1 tsp. coarsely ground black pepper
- 8 tbsp. Tamari® Low Sodium soy sauce
- 2 tbsp. minced garlic
- 1 oz. freshly grated ginger root
- 1 tbsp. ground mustard seed
- 1 tbsp. extra virgin olive oil

PREPARATION:

1. Season the flank steak by rubbing with coarsely ground black pepper.
2. With a sharp knife, cut into steak diagonally in both directions, creating a diamond pattern in the meat to allow the marinade to penetrate more thoroughly.
3. In a large Ziploc bag place low sodium soy sauce, minced garlic, 1/2 cup minced onion, grated ginger root, and ground mustard seed. Close Ziploc bag and shake gently to mix marinate. Add flank steak to marinade mixture, close bag, shake, and refrigerate for several hours or overnight for a more tender steak.

4. Coat cooking surface of extra large skillet with olive oil, and preheat skillet over medium heat.
5. Add flank steak to skillet and sear for 2 minutes. Cover and cook an additional 3 minutes.
6. Turn steak over and sear for 2 minutes. Add mushrooms, cover and cook for 8 minutes, stirring occasionally, for medium rare. Longer cooking times help make flank steak more tender.
7. Remove steak and let rest covered on a warm plate for 10 minutes before cutting.
8. Cut steak diagonally into eight equal portions; place each portion on a warm serving plate.
9. Distribute vegetables equally over the tops of each of the 8 portions.

TANGY TURKEY BREAST ROLL-UP TO GO

YIELD: Serves 1

Per portion:

GI: 50
GL: 8

CALORIES: 375; Carbohydrates: 20g; Fiber: 11g; Protein: 39g; Fat: 14g; Saturated Fats: 4g; Sodium: 644mg

INGREDIENTS:

- 3 oz. roasted turkey breast, sliced
- 1 oz. sliced avocado
- 1 slice bacon
- 1 tbsp. thinly sliced sweet onion
- 1 slice (1 oz.) low-fat cheddar cheese
- 1 Mission® Brand Carb Balance Low Carb Tortilla
- 1 oz. slice fresh tomato
- 1 oz. fresh alfalfa sprouts, rinsed and gently patted dry
- 1 tbsp. low sodium diet mayonnaise

PREPARATION:

1. In a small skillet, fry bacon slice until crisp. Place on paper towel to drain excess fat.
2. Wrap tortilla in damp paper towel. Microwave tortilla on high setting for one minute.
3. Remove tortilla from paper towel and place on a piece of parchment paper cut to just a bit larger in size than the tortilla.
4. Spread mayonnaise over tortilla. Add sliced turkey breast, cheese, bacon, alfalfa sprouts, tomato, and onion.
5. Fold tortilla end over filling; roll up and form a burrito. Fold up one end of parchment paper and roll up as you did to form burrito.

VEAL SCALOPPINI

YIELD: Serves 3

Per portion:

GI: 40
GL: 2.96

CALORIES: 292.33; Carbohydrates: 7.41g; Fiber: 2.83; Protein: 27.69g; Fat: 17.51g; Saturated Fat: 3.43g; Sodium: 572.66mg

INGREDIENTS:

- 3/4 lb. boneless veal leg top round steak, cut 1/4 inch thick
- 2 cups fresh mushrooms, sliced
- 3 oz. white cooking wine
- 2 tbsp. water
- 1 tbsp. Bragg® Liquid Aminos
- 1 tbsp. snipped fresh parsley
- 1/8 tsp. freshly ground black peppercorns, to taste
- 1 tbsp. paprika
- 1 tsp. tarragon
- 1 oz. Bobs Red Mill® almond meal flour
- 1 tbsp. unsalted organic butter
- 1 tbsp. extra virgin olive oil

PREPARATION:

1. Trim off any visible fat from veal steak. Cut veal into 6 equal pieces. Pound steaks (you can cover the veal steaks with waxed paper and use a rolling pin) to 1/8-inch thickness. (A dinner serving is two pieces.)
2. Combine almond meal flour, paprika, and tarragon in a small mixing bowl.
3. Dredge veal in flour mixture to lightly coat surface.
4. Coat the cooking surface of a 12-inch skillet with olive oil. Preheat skillet over medium heat.

5. Cook veal for 2-3 minutes or until the meat is no longer pink, turning once. Remove from skillet; cover veal to keep warm.
6. For sauce, using the same skillet with remaining drippings, add the white cooking wine, water, butter and pepper. Stir in the mushrooms.
7. Bring to boiling, stirring to scrape up browned bits from bottom of the skillet. Continue to simmer gently, uncovered, about 3 minutes or until most of the liquid has evaporated to form a nice gravy. Remove from heat.
8. Add Bragg® Liquid Aminos to mixture, and stir to combine.
9. Arrange veal equally onto 3 serving plates. Pour 1/3 of sauce over each serving and sprinkle with snipped parsley.

BEEFY SAUTE' & VEGETABLES

YIELD: Serves 1

Per portion:

GI: 40
GL: 9

CALORIES: 583; Carbohydrates: 22.5g; Fiber: 4g; Protein: 41g; Fat: 44g; Saturated Fats: 12g; Sodium: 664mg

INGREDIENTS:

- 6 oz. very thinly sliced beef flank steak, trimmed of visible fat
- 1/2 cup mushrooms, rinsed, dried and sliced in half
- 1/2 cup zucchini, sliced into 1/2 inch pieces
- 1/4 cup sliced onion
- 1/4 cup carrot, sliced lengthwise into spears
- 1 tbsp. canola oil
- 1 tbsp. oyster sauce
- 1 tbsp. apple cider vinegar

PREPARATION:

1. Combine canola oil, oyster sauce, and vinegar in covered container and shake vigorously.
2. Place beef slices in mixture and marinate for 1 hour.
3. Heat sauté pan over medium heat and pour marinated beef and marinade mixture into pan.
4. Place all vegetables on top of this mixture. Cover and cook for 10 minutes over medium heat.
5. Cook, uncovered for another 5 minutes, stirring occasionally.

VEGGIE MEAT LOAF

YIELD: Serves 5

Per portion:

GI: 51
GL: 8.72

CALORIES: 174.7; Carbohydrates: 17.1g; Fiber: 5.4g; Protein: 14.2; Fat: 5g; Saturated Fats: .6g; Sodium: 394.4mg

INGREDIENTS:

- One 12 oz. package Smart Ground® Mexican Style Veggie Protein Crumbles
- 1 cup raw Portobello mushrooms, sliced thin
- 4 oz. finely chopped onion
- 1 tsp. chopped garlic
- 2 slices 100% Whole Grain Bread (produced by Natural Ovens,® USA) bread, dipped in water and squeezed to remove excess water
- 2 tbsp. tomato sauce
- 1 medium egg, lightly beaten
- 2 tbsp. finely chopped fresh parsley
- 1/2 tsp. dried basil leaves
- 1/4 tsp. dried thyme
- 1/2 tsp. dried oregano leaves
- 1/2 tsp. Worcestershire sauce
- 1 tsp. canola oil

PREPARATION:

1. Preheat oven to 350 degrees.
2. In a medium sized mixing bowl, combine squeezed bread slices, onion, garlic, tomato sauce, beaten egg, basil, thyme, oregano, and Worcestershire Sauce. Whisk together to combine thoroughly.

3. Add veggie protein crumbles and mushrooms and mix well.
4. Coat cooking surface of 9x 5 X 2 inch loaf pan with canola oil.
5. Place Smart Ground® mixture in oiled loaf pan, and cover tightly with aluminum foil.
6. Bake in 350 degree oven for about 45 minutes.
7. Slice meatloaf into 5 equal portions, placing each on a warm serving plate.

YUMMY PORK STIR-FRY

YIELD: Serves 2

Per portion:

GI: 40
GL: 6.62

CALORIES: 363.75; Carbohydrates: 16.56g; Fiber: 6.5; Protein: 32.25g; Fat: 17.5g; Saturated fats: 1g; Sodium: 458.25mg

INGREDIENTS:

- 7 oz. pork tenderloin, cut into strips
- 3 cups fresh snap green beans
- 4 oz. carrots, sliced
- 4 oz. celery, cut into bite-sized chunks
- 2 tbsp. garlic, minced
- 1 tbsp. Tamari® Low Sodium soy sauce
- 2 tbsp. extra virgin olive oil
- 2 tbsp. water

PREPARATION:

1. Heat 1 tbsp. of the olive oil in a wok or large skillet over medium heat.
2. Add pork strips and garlic, cook, covered for 40 minutes or until well done. Remove the pork strips from the pan and set aside.
3. Heat the other 1 tbsp. of olive oil and add celery and carrot pieces and the green beans. Cook, covered until vegetables become crisp-tender (about 5 minutes). Add 2 tbsp. water to prevent scorching the vegetables, if needed.
4. Add the pork strips back to the skillet of vegetables along with the soy sauce.
5. Cook for about two minutes more, stirring occasionally.
6. Distribute pork, vegetables and sauce evenly onto 2 warm serving plates.

PECAN CRUNCH ROAST SALMON

YIELD: Serves 4

Per portion:

GI: <1
GL: <1

CALORIES: 359.5 Carbohydrates: 2.53g; Fiber: 1.63; Protein: 32.75g; Fat: 25.75g; Saturated fats: 2.18g; Sodium: 122mg

INGREDIENTS:

- 4 salmon filets (5 ounces each)
- 2 tbsp. almond meal flour
- 1 tbsp. Dijon mustard
- 1 tbsp. fresh parsley, chopped
- 2 tbsp. chopped pecans
- 1 tbsp. grated parmesan cheese
- 2 tbsp. extra virgin olive oil

PREPARATION:

1. Preheat oven to 400 degrees.
2. Spread 1 tbsp. olive oil over bottom of 9 X 13 inch glass baking dish.
3. Rinse salmon and pat dry. Place in baking dish with skin side down.
4. Combine 1 tbsp. olive oil and mustard, and brush mixture on top of salmon.
5. Combine almond meal flour, chopped pecans, and parmesan cheese. Distribute mixture evenly on top of 4 salmon fillets, pressing into mustard sauce.
6. Bake for 10 minutes or until salmon flakes easily with a fork.
7. Distribute evenly among 4 serving plates.

SHRIMP AND CHICKEN STIR-FRY

YIELD: Serves 4

Per portion:

GI: 40
GL: 6.2

CALORIES: 286; Carbohydrates: 15.5g; Fiber: 12.5g; Protein: 39g; Fat: 4.5g; Saturated Fats: .5g; Sodium: 473mg

INGREDIENTS:

- 12 oz. medium sized raw shrimp, shell removed and deveined
- 12 oz. skinless, boneless chicken breast, cubed
- 4 cups fresh broccoli flowerets
- 1/2 cup carrot, julienned
- 1/2 cup sliced celery
- 4 tbsp. Chef Mate Hoisin Sauce®
- 1 tbsp. extra virgin olive oil

PREPARATION:

1. Heat oil in a wok or large skillet over medium heat, being sure to coat cooking surface.
2. Add cubed chicken. Cook chicken for about 15 minutes until browned, stirring occasionally. Remove chicken from wok and cover to keep warm.
3. Add raw shrimp. Cook for about four minutes or until translucent, stirring occasionally.
4. Return chicken back into wok.
5. Add broccoli and carrots. Continue to cook until shrimp and chicken are lightly browned and vegetables are crisp-tender.
6. Add Hoisin Sauce to the wok. Turn off the heat. Stir well to combine ingredients.
7. Distribute chicken, shrimp, and vegetables equally onto 4 serving plates.

FINISHING TOUCHES TO YOUR MEAL

SIDE DISHES

I LOVE PARMESAN TOMATOES

YIELD: Serves 4

Per portion:

GI: 50
GL: 1.75

CALORIES: 115.5; Carbohydrates: 3.5g; Fiber: 1g; Protein: 3g; Fat: 9g; Saturated Fats: 2.25g; Sodium: 80.5mg

INGREDIENTS:

- 2 cups fresh whole red ripe tomatoes
- 4 tbsp. Parmesan cheese
- 2 ½ tbsp. extra virgin olive oil
- 1 tbsp. minced garlic
- 1 tbsp. fresh parsley
- ¼ tsp. freshly ground black peppercorns, to taste

PREPARATION:

1. Rinse parsley and tomatoes well; blot dry with a clean soft towel. Chop parsley and set aside.
2. Coat a baking dish with 1 tbsp. olive oil.
3. Slice the tomatoes into 1/4 inch thick slices and place on the baking dish.
4. Mix together 1 1/2 tbsp. olive oil, chopped parsley, garlic, and a dash of freshly ground black peppercorns.
5. Drizzle this mixture over the sliced tomatoes, and sprinkle with the Parmesan cheese.
6. Place under broiler and cook for 5 minutes to melt the parmesan cheese.
7. Evenly distribute onto 4 serving plates.

CAULIFLOWER AND CHEESE

YIELD: Serves 2

Per portion:

GI: 40
GL: 2.4

CALORIES: 146; Carbohydrates: 6g; Fiber: 3g; Protein: 7.5g; Fat: 2g; Saturated Fats: 1g; Sodium: 201mg

INGREDIENTS:

- 2 cups cauliflower flowerets
- 2 oz. low-fat Colby cheese, shredded
- 1/8 tsp. freshly ground black peppercorns, to taste

PREPARATION:

1. In a medium saucepan, bring 1 cup of water to a boil. Add 1 cup of fresh cauliflower flowerets. Boil for 3 minutes.
2. Pour off excess water, reserving 2 tbsp. of water. Pour cauliflower in a microwavable small bowl. Sprinkle with freshly ground black peppercorns. Top with Colby cheese.
3. Microwave for about 1 minute on medium heat until cheese melts.
4. Divide equally onto two serving plates.

CABBAGE AND APPLE SALAD

YIELD: Serves 1

Per Portion:

GI: 40
GL: 7

CALORIES: 90.50; Carbohydrates: 17.50g; Fiber: 2g; Protein: 1.5g; Fat: g; Saturated Fats: g; Sodium: 52mg

INGREDIENTS:

- 1/2 cup shredded fresh green cabbage
- 1/2 cup golden delicious apple, coarsely chopped
- 1/4 cup coarsely chopped purple onion
- 1/4 cup The Greek Gods® Traditional Plain Greek Yogurt (in the green container)

PREPARATION:

1. Combine all ingredients in mixing bowl. Cover.
2. Refrigerate 20 minutes, to meld flavors before serving.

STEAMED GREEN BEANS WITH ALMONDS

YIELD: Serves 1

Per portion:

GI: 40
GL: 4.48

CALORIES: 217; Carbohydrates: 11.2g; Fiber: 4.4g; Protein: 4.2g; Fat: 18.9g; Saturated Fats: 2.5g; Sodium: 6.2mg

INGREDIENTS:

- 1 cup fresh green beans—snap or string, rinsed well
- 1 tbsp. extra virgin olive oil
- 1 tbsp. sliced almonds
- 1/8 tsp. freshly ground black peppercorns, to taste

PREPARATION:

1. Place the green beans in a stainless steel colander in a large stainless steel Dutch oven containing 2 inches of water. Cover. Bring water to a boil over medium high heat. Steam green beans until just crisp tender, for about 3 minutes.
2. Place green beans on serving plate.
3. Sprinkle olive oil over the green beans.
4. Sprinkle with sliced almonds and freshly ground black peppercorns.

TANGY TOMATO & CUCUMBER SALAD

YIELD: Serves 1

Per portion:

GI: 50
GL: 1.38

CALORIES: 13; Carbohydrates: 2.75g; Fiber: .2g; Protein: .1g; Fat: 0g; Saturated Fats: 0g; Sodium: 4.5mg

INGREDIENTS:

- 1/4 cup red ripe tomatoes, sliced
- 1/4 cup peeled and sliced cucumber
- 1 tbsp. vinegar (apple cider, balsamic or red wine)
- 2 drops liquid stevia

PREPARATION:

1. In a small bowl, combine 1 tbsp. vinegar, 1 tsp. water and stevia.
2. Add sliced tomato and cucumber to vinegar mixture. Stir gently to combine ingredients and serve

CHICKPEA SHUFFLE

YIELD: Serves 6

Per portion:

GI: 42
GL: 8.54

CALORIES: 106.5; Carbohydrates: 20.33g; Fiber: 4.8g; Protein: 2.83g; Fat: 3g; Saturated Fats: .04g; Sodium: 199.66mg

INGREDIENTS:

- One 12 oz. can chickpeas, drained
- 8 oz. celery, 8 oz. broccoli, and 8 oz. carrot sticks
- 1 oz. freshly squeezed lemon juice
- 1 tsp. paprika
- 1 tbsp. extra virgin olive oil
- 1 tsp. minced garlic

PREPARATION:

1. Drain chickpeas and mash well with fork in a small mixing bowl.
2. Add olive oil, lemon juice, garlic and paprika.
3. Mix very thoroughly; then refrigerate 20 minutes.
4. Wash, rinse, dry, and slice celery, broccoli and carrot, to provide 6 servings of each.
5. Divide vegetables evenly among 6 serving plates.
6. Place an equal serving of chickpea mixture in the center of each of the 6 plates. Arrange fresh vegetables around chickpea center.

PARISIAN ASPARAGUS

YIELD: Serves 4

Per portion:

GI: 40
GL: .8

CALORIES: 215.5; Carbohydrates: 2g; Fiber: 2g; Protein: 4.25g; Fat: 17g; Saturated Fats: 7g; Sodium: 445.75mg

INGREDIENTS:

- 1 pound small fresh spears of asparagus
- 1/2 cup grated Parmesan cheese
- 1 tsp. minced garlic
- 3 ½ oz. Campbell's® Low Sodium Chicken broth
- 1 tbsp. freshly squeezed lemon juice
- 2 tbsp. extra virgin olive oil
- 1/4 cup chopped fresh parsley

PREPARATION:

1. Rinse asparagus well. Gently break off woody ends, which will snap off naturally.
2. Place asparagus in a stainless steel colander in a large Dutch oven containing 2 inches of water over medium high heat. Bring water to a boil. Cover and steam asparagus for 3-4 minutes (or less, to taste) until just crisp tender.
3. In a small sauce pan, heat 2 tbsp. olive oil over medium heat until it shimmers. Add the garlic, and cook, stirring constantly until the garlic becomes aromatic, for about one minute.
4. Add the chicken broth and parsley, and cook for an additional minute.

5. Whisk in the lemon juice, mixing for about 30 seconds. Remove from heat.
6. Distribute asparagus evenly among 4 serving plates; spoon 1/4 of sauce over each serving of asparagus and sprinkle each serving with 1/4 of Parmesan cheese.

BROCCOLI CASHEW CHEDDAR SALAD

YIELD: Serves 5

Per portion:

GI: 40
GL: 2.46

CALORIES: 129; Carbohydrates: 6.14g; Fiber: 5.2g; Protein: 7.32g; Fat: 6g; Saturated Fats: 2.49g; Sodium: 209.4mg

INGREDIENTS:

- 3 cups fresh broccoli crowns, cut into 1/2 inch pieces
- 1/4 cup chopped raw cashews
- 1/4 cup chopped red onion
- 1/4 cup shredded cheddar cheese
- 1/4 cup light sour cream
- 1/4 cup light mayonnaise
- 1/4 tsp. finely chopped fresh ginger
- 1/4 tsp. freshly ground black peppercorns

PREPARATION:

1. Combine light sour cream, light mayonnaise, cheddar cheese, finely chopped fresh ginger and freshly ground black peppercorns in a small bowl, stirring well. Chill in refrigerator.
2. Combine the broccoli, cashews and onions in a medium sized bowl, stirring to mix well.
3. Add the dressing mixture to the broccoli mixture, stirring well to coat all the dry ingredients with the sour cream mixture.
4. Refrigerate covered for several hours or overnight before serving.
5. Distribute evenly among 5 serving plates.

ARTICHOKE SALAD

YIELD: Serves 2

Per portion:

GI: 40
GL: 3.6

CALORIES: 156; Carbohydrates: 9g; Fiber: 4g; Protein: 3g; Fat: 13g; Saturated Fats: 2g; Sodium: 119mg

INGREDIENTS:

- 8 frozen artichoke hearts
- Juice of 1/2 red grapefruit
- 1/4 cup extra virgin olive oil
- 1 tsp. minced garlic
- 1/4 cup chopped fresh mint
- 1 tbsp. feta cheese
- 1 cup romaine lettuce

PREPARATION:

1. Defrost the artichoke hearts and place in a 2 cup jar.
2. Add the olive oil, minced garlic, fresh mint, and the grapefruit juice. Place cover on jar.
3. Shake vigorously and store in fridge while preparing the lettuce.
4. Rinse the romaine lettuce and gently pat dry.
5. Tear the lettuce into 2 salad bowls or onto the sides of 2 plates, leaving room for your choice of entrée.
6. When ready to serve, arrange half of artichoke mixture of top of each lettuce bed.

CRISPY CUCUMBER ONION SALAD

YIELD: Serves 6

Per portion:

GI: 40
GL: 1.72

CALORIES: 36; Carbohydrates: 4.3g; Fiber: 4g; Protein: 0.5g; Fat: 0.1g; Saturated Fats: 0g; Sodium: 4mg

INGREDIENTS:

- 2 ½ cups cucumber, peeled and thinly sliced
- 1/2 cup red or white sweet Spanish onion, thinly sliced
- 1/2 cup apple cider vinegar
- 1 tbsp. chives, finely chopped
- 1/2 tsp. fresh ginger, finely grated
- 1/2 tsp. dried oregano leaves, crushed
- 1/2 tsp. freshly ground black peppercorns, to taste

PREPARATION:

1. Combine last five ingredients in a medium sized bowl.
2. Add the cucumber and onion. Mix well. Cover.
3. Refrigerate for several hours or overnight to blend flavors.

ORIENTAL COLLARD GREENS

YIELD: Serves 4

Per portion:

GI: 40
GL: 3.2

CALORIES: 63; Carbohydrates: 8g; Fiber: 4.1g; Protein: 3.1g; Fat: 2.7g; Saturated Fats: 2g; Sodium: 174mg

INGREDIENTS:

- 1 pound fresh collard greens
- Juice of 1/2 red grapefruit
- 1 tsp. freshly grated orange rind
- 2 tsp. dark (toasted) sesame oil
- 2 tsp. crushed garlic
- 1 tbsp. reduced sodium soy sauce

PREPARATION:

1. Place the collard greens in a colander, and rinse thoroughly under running cold water. Shake off excess water. Stack the leaves onto a cutting board and slice into 1/4 inch strips.
2. Place the sliced greens in a large deep skillet over medium high heat, and add the grapefruit juice and orange rind.
3. Cover, and cook, tossing frequently, for about 4 minutes, until the greens turn bright green and become crisp-tender. (You can add a bit of water if skillet becomes dry.)
4. Move the greens to one side of the skillet and add the garlic and oil. Sauté for a few seconds to liberate the fragrance, and the garlic begins to turn translucent.

5. Remove skillet from the heat and sprinkle soy sauce over the top of the garlic. Toss greens with garlic-soy sauce mixture to coat them with the sauce.
6. Distribute evenly among 4 serving plates.

BROCCOLI GARLIC CASHEW CRUNCH

YIELD: Serves 4

Per portion:

**GI: 40
GL: 4**

CALORIES: 159; Carbohydrates: 10g; Fiber 1.68g; Fat: 8.17g; Saturated Fat: 2.5g; Protein: 3.84g; Sodium: 52.5mg

INGREDIENTS:

- 2 cups rinsed, sliced broccoli crowns (cut larger stems in half for faster cooking)
- 2 oz. raw cashews, chopped
- 2 tbsp. minced fresh garlic
- 1/4 cup chopped onion
- 2 tbsp. unsalted butter
- 2 tbsp. water (from steamer pot)
- 1 tsp. freshly ground black peppercorns, to taste

PREPARATION:

1. Place broccoli and onion in a stainless steel colander in a large stainless steel Dutch oven containing 2 inches of water over medium high heat. Bring water to a boil. Cover and steam vegetables for 5-8 minutes until just crisp tender. Remove cooked vegetables to platter.
2. In the same pan, after pouring out all but 2 tsp. of the water, add butter, garlic, and black pepper. Cook over medium-low heat, stirring until butter melts.
3. Distribute broccoli–onion mixture evenly onto 4 serving plates.
4. Pour the butter-spice mixture evenly over each of the 4 servings.
5. Top each serving with ½ ounce of chopped cashews.

GOLDEN CABBAGE AND ONIONS

YIELD: Serves 4

Per portion:

GI: 40
GL: 5.32

CALORIES: 197.9; Carbohydrates: 13.35g; Fiber: 3.4g; Protein: 3.08g; Fat: 6.75g; Saturated Fat: .9g; Sodium: 8.5mg

INGREDIENTS:

- 2 cups cabbage, core removed, cut into 1/2 inch slices
- 2 cups yellow onion, cut into 1/2 inch slices
- 2 tbsp. extra virgin olive oil
- 1/4 cup water
- 1/4 tsp. dried thyme

PREPARATION:

1. Coat cooking surface of large skillet with olive oil, and place skillet over medium heat.
2. Add the onions and thyme. Cover and cook for about 3 minutes, stirring occasionally.
3. Add the cabbage and water, and reduce heat to medium-low. Cover and continue cooking for another 10 minutes or more, stirring occasionally, until the cabbage and onion are tender. Add a little more water as necessary to avoid burning the vegetables.
4. Distribute evenly among 4 serving plates with entre' of your choice.

POPEYE MUSHROOM CAPS

YIELD: Serves 8

Per portion:

GI: 55
GL: 5.26

CALORIES: 87.25; Carbohydrates: 9.56g; Fiber: 1.71g; Protein: 7.13g; Fat: 3.63g; Saturated Fats: .5g; Sodium: 142.94mg

INGREDIENTS:

- 1 lb. large mushrooms (about 24)
- 1 package frozen chopped spinach (10 oz.) thawed and drained well (Place in a strainer basket and press spinach against sides to remove extra water.)
- 12 oz. Mori-Nu® Extra Firm Tofu, mashed
- 1 slice Healthy Choice® 7 Grain bread, air dried (or oven dried on low heat setting) and grated
- 3 oz. scallions, very finely chopped
- 3 oz. celery, very finely chopped
- 2 tbsp. mayonnaise
- 2 tbsp. Parmesan cheese, grated
- 1 tbsp. minced garlic
- 1 tbsp. fresh sage, very finely chopped
- 1 tbsp. fresh parsley, very finely chopped
- 1 tbsp. fresh basil, very finely chopped
- 1 tsp. Dijon mustard
- 2 tbsp. extra virgin olive oil

PREPARATION:

1. Preheat oven to 350 degrees.

2. Rinse mushrooms well, dry with paper towel. Remove and chop stems; set aside in serving bowl.
3. Coat cooking surface of medium sized skillet with 1 tbsp. of olive oil. Sauté chopped mushroom stems, garlic, celery, scallions, tofu, basil, Dijon mustard and sage over medium-low heat for 2 minutes, stirring frequently. Remove from heat and let cool for 10 minutes, stirring after 5 minutes to liberate heat.
4. Combine spinach, bread crumbs, Parmesan cheese and mayonnaise in a mixing bowl. Add to chopped mushroom mixture and mix well.
5. Coat baking surface of 11 X 8 X 1/2 inch baking dish with 1 tbsp. olive oil. Spoon spinach mixture into mushroom caps; place stuffed mushroom caps into baking dish.
6. Sprinkle parsley over tops of stuffed mushrooms.
7. Bake in preheated 350 degree oven for 15 minutes.
8. Distribute stuffed mushroom caps evenly among 6 serving plates.

JICAMA ZUCCHINI SALAD

YIELD: Serves 4

Per portion:

GI: 50
GL: 2.05

CALORIES: 42; Carbohydrates: 4.1g; Fiber: 4g; Protein: .5g; Fat: 1.8g; Saturated Fats: 0.2g; Sodium: 2mg

INGREDIENTS:

- 1 cup jicama, julienned
- 1/4 cup zucchini, julienned
- 1 tbsp. red onion, finely chopped
- 1/4 cup freshly peeled orange segments, sliced
- 1 tbsp. juice from orange
- 4 large fresh romaine lettuce leaves
- 1/2 tsp. freshly ground black peppercorns, to taste
- 1 tbsp. extra virgin olive oil
- 1 tbsp. cilantro, finely chopped
- 1 tbsp. freshly squeezed lime juice

PREPARATION:

1. Combine the last five ingredients in a medium sized bowl.
2. Add the jicama, zucchini, red onion, sliced orange segments and juice.
3. Gently combine all ingredients.
4. Rinse the romaine lettuce and gently pat dry.
5. Arrange lettuce on 4 plates, and top each with 1/4 of Jicama Zucchini Salad.

SAUTEED VEGETABLES

YIELD: Serves 4

Per portion:

GI: 40
GL: 5.40

CALORIES: 59.75; Carbohydrates: 13.5g; Fiber: 3g; Protein: 3g; Fat: 8.05g; Saturated Fats: .7g; Sodium: 11.25mg

INGREDIENTS:

- 2 zucchini squash, cut into thick 4-inch strips
- 1 large onion, sliced
- 1 oz. pine nuts
- 1 tbsp. minced garlic
- 1 tbsp. sliced shallots
- 1 tbsp. canola oil

PREPARATION:

1. Add canola oil to a large skillet.
2. Place skillet over medium-high heat.
3. Add onion. Cook for about 1 minute.
4. Add zucchini squash strips, pine nuts, shallots, and minced garlic. Cover and cook for about 3 minutes, stirring occasionally, until vegetables become slightly tender.
5. Distribute evenly among 4 serving plates.

TEXAS SLAW

YIELD: Serves 3

Per portion:

GI: 40
GL: 1.2

CALORIES: 82.6; Carbohydrates: 3g; Fiber: .66g; Protein: .33g; Fat: 6g; Saturated Fats: .66g; Sodium: 160.3mg

INGREDIENTS:

- One 10 oz. bag finely shredded cabbage
- 1/4 cup light mayonnaise
- 2 drops liquid stevia
- 1/4 cup apple cider vinegar
- 1 tsp. ground celery seed

PREPARATION:

1. Combine light mayonnaise, stevia, apple cider vinegar, and celery seed in a large mixing bowl.
2. Add fine shred cabbage and mix well.
3. Cover and refrigerate for 2 hours or until ready to serve.
4. Stir just before serving, and distribute evenly among 3 serving plates.

SPAGHETTI SQUASH VINAIGRETTE

YIELD: Serves 2

Per portion:

GI: 40
GL: 5.63

CALORIES: 189.56; Carbohydrates: 14.07g; Fiber: 1.51; Protein: .87g; Fat: 14.26g; Saturated Fat: 2g; Sodium: 26.5mg

INGREDIENTS

- 1 yellow winter spaghetti squash (2 cups, cooked)
- 4 oz. sliced onion
- 1 oz. balsamic vinegar
- 1 oz. fresh lime juice
- 1/4 tsp. freshly ground black peppercorns
- 2 tbsp. extra virgin olive oil
- 2 sprigs of fresh cilantro

PREPARATION

1. Rinse squash, remove stem and place in microwave oven.
2. Microwave on high for about 15 minutes, turning as necessary, until squash is tender when pierced with a fork.
3. Put olive oil, onion, balsamic vinegar, lemon juice and pepper into a small saucepan. Cover and heat over medium heat until onion is soft and lightly browned, stirring frequently, for about 8 minutes, adding 1 tbsp. water as needed to prevent onion from scorching. Remove from heat. Cover and keep warm.
4. When squash becomes tender, place on a cutting board and slice in half. (Put on oven mitts to protect your hands, as squash will be very hot.) Using a fork, scrape inside tender squash "spaghetti" strings into a mixing bowl.

5. Pour vinaigrette mixture over squash. Mix gently.
6. Divide evenly onto 2 serving plates. Garnish each serving with a sprig of with fresh cilantro.

SUMPTUOUS RAINBOW SWISS CHARD

YIELD: Serves 3

Per portion:

GI: 40
GL: 4.4

CALORIES: 166.3; Carbohydrates: 11g; Fiber: 4.3g; Protein: 5.6g; Fat: 15.6g; Saturated Fats: .3g; Sodium: 208.6mg

INGREDIENTS:

- 1 large bunch of rainbow Swiss chard leaves, washed, rinsed, towel dried, and chopped (1 cup)
- 1/4 cup pine nuts
- 1 tbsp. minced garlic
- 1 tbsp. apple cider vinegar
- 1 tsp. extra virgin olive oil
- 1 tsp. freshly ground black peppercorns, to taste
- 2 tbsp. fresh shallots, sliced

PREPARATION:

1. In a large skillet, toast the pine nuts over low medium heat, stirring frequently, for about 2 to 3 minutes. Remove pine nuts and set aside.
2. Coat the same skillet with olive oil, and preheat over low medium heat.
3. Add shallots and garlic, cover, and steam until tender, about 2 minutes.
4. Turn the heat up to medium. Add the chopped rainbow Swiss chard and ground black peppercorns. Cover and cook for 5 to 7 minutes until rainbow Swiss chard is just barely tender.

5. Add the apple cider vinegar to the skillet and cover. Allow the rainbow Swiss chard to steam until tender, and most of the liquid has evaporated, about 5 minutes.
6. Remove rainbow Swiss chard equally to 3 serving plates; garnish each serving with one third of toasted pine nuts.

STIR-FRY SWEET & SOUR FRESH SNAP GREEN BEANS

YIELD: Serves 4

Per portion:

GI: 40
GL: 3.2

CALORIES: 70; Carbohydrates: 8g; Fiber: 2g; Protein: 2.5g; Fat: 4.25g; Saturated Fats: .75g; Sodium: 632mg

INGREDIENTS:

- 1 pound fresh snap green beans
- 8 oz. can water chestnuts, drained and sliced
- 1 tbsp. minced garlic
- 2 tbsp. Tamari® soy sauce
- 2 tbsp. hoisin sauce
- 2 tbsp. apple cider vinegar
- 2 tbsp. peanut oil
- 1 tbsp. dark sesame oil
- 1 tsp. hot pepper sauce, to taste

PREPARATION:

1. Place beans in stainless steel colander and rinse under cool water.
2. Pop off ends, leaving beans whole.
3. Place stainless steel colander of beans into stainless steel Dutch oven with 2 inches of water on the bottom.
4. Place over high heat; bring to a boil and cover, allowing beans to steam for just 30 seconds.
5. Turn off heat, and remove colander of beans to counter.

6. In a small bowl, combine Tamari® soy sauce, apple cider vinegar, hoisin sauce, and hot pepper sauce.
7. In a wok or large skillet, put 2 tsp. of peanut oil, being sure to coat cooking surface, and place over medium-high heat. Add green beans and garlic.
8. Stir-fry bean and garlic mixture for 2 minutes.
9. Add the soy sauce mixture, and cook, stirring constantly for another 2 minutes.
10. Gently stir in the water chestnuts and drizzle with sesame oil. Stir gently to combine all ingredients.
11. Divide mixture evenly onto 4 serving plates; serve immediately

SPINACH SOYBEAN SOUFFLE'

YIELD: Serves 4

Per portion:

GI: 40
GL: 3.6

CALORIES: 230.5; Carbohydrates: 9g; Fiber: 21g; Protein: 16.75g; Fat: 15.5g; Saturated Fats: 1g; Sodium: 378mg

INGREDIENTS:

- 1 package (10 oz.) frozen chopped spinach; thawed and squeezed to remove excess liquid (Place in a strainer basket and press spinach against the sides to remove extra water.)
- 1/2 cup soybeans (frozen are called edamame, but do remove the outer shell after they are thawed)
- 2 extra-large eggs – organic if available
- 1/2 cup water
- 1 tbsp. extra virgin olive oil
- 1 tsp. baking powder
- 1 tsp. minced garlic
- 1 tbsp. finely chopped onion
- 1 tsp. Dijon mustard
- 2 tbsp. grated Parmesan cheese

PREPARATION:

1. Preheat oven to 375 degrees.
2. Using an electric mixer, beat eggs well in a large mixing bowl.
3. Add remaining ingredients, with the exception of spinach and soy beans. Beat thoroughly with electric mixer to combine all ingredients well.
4. Gently fold in spinach and soybeans.
5. Coat cooking surface of 8 inch square baking dish with olive oil.

6. Pour spinach mixture into baking dish. Bake uncovered for about 40 minutes, or until knife inserted into center comes out clean.
7. Slice soufflé into 4 equal portions and place each portion on a warm serving plate.

SAVORY KALE AND LEEKS

YIELD: Serves 2

Per portion:

GI: 40
GL: 4.8

CALORIES: 116.75; Carbohydrates: 12g; Fiber: 1.50g; Protein: 1.5g; Fat: 7g; Saturated Fats: 1g; Sodium: 32mg

INGREDIENTS:

- 1 cup kale, rinsed, chopped, and compacted
- 1 leek, rinsed and sliced into rounds
- 1/4 cup low sodium chicken or vegetable broth
- 1 tbsp. minced fresh garlic
- 1 tbsp. freshly squeezed lemon juice
- 1 tbsp. extra virgin olive oil
- 1 tbsp. apple cider vinegar
- 1 tsp. freshly ground black peppercorns, to taste

PREPARATION:

1. Heat broth in a stainless steel skillet over medium low heat.
2. Add the chopped kale and sliced leak, cover and simmer gently over medium low heat for 7 to 8 minutes, stirring at least every two minutes. You can add a bit of water if vegetables become dry.
3. Toss with the minced garlic and lemon juice. Add the olive oil, the freshly ground black peppercorns and apple cider vinegar, stirring well to combine ingredients.
4. Divide mixture evenly onto 2 serving plates. Serve immediately for finest flavor.

WALDORF SALAD

YIELD: Serves 6

Per portion:

GI: 40
GL: 3.4

CALORIES: 116.25; Carbohydrates: 8.5g; Fiber: 1g; Protein: 1.67g; Fat: 8.67g;
Saturated Fats: 1.67g; Sodium: 29mg

INGREDIENTS:

- 2 cups coarsely chopped golden delicious apples
- 4 oz. celery, sliced into 1/2 inch rounds
- 2 oz. walnuts, coarsely chopped
- 2 oz. low sodium diet mayonnaise
- 2 oz. reduced fat sour cream
- 1 tbsp. freshly squeezed lemon juice

PREPARATION:

1. Mix mayonnaise, sour cream, and freshly squeezed lemon juice in a medium-sized bowl.
2. Add coarsely chopped walnuts, and combine thoroughly.
3. Fold in apples and celery.
4. Cover and refrigerate for several hours or overnight.
5. Divide mixture evenly among 6 serving plates.

SPICED CHINESE BROCCOLI

YIELD: Serves 4

Per portion:

GI: 40
GL: 3.42

CALORIES: 141.5; Carbohydrates: 8.56g; Fiber: 5.8g; Protein: 6.68g; Fat: 5.75g; Saturated Fat: 1.5g; Sodium: 169.25mg.

INGREDIENTS:

- 2 cups small Chinese broccoli flowerets, rinsed
- 2 oz. soy nuts, crushed
- 1 tsp. soy sauce
- 1 tsp. hoisin sauce
- 1 tsp. five spice powder
- 2 tbsp. Land O Lakes® Spreadable Butter with Canola Oil

PREPARATION:

1. Steam broccoli in stainless steel colander in covered stainless steel Dutch oven over 2 inches of boiling water on medium heat until stems are tender (about 5 minutes). Remove cooked broccoli to mixing bowl.
2. Using the same Dutch oven, after pouring out the water, add butter, soy sauce, five-spice powder, and 2 tsp. of water. Cook over medium to low heat, stirring until butter melts. Turn off the heat.
3. Add broccoli back to the Dutch oven and mix gently with the sauce to coat the broccoli with the sauce.
4. Divide broccoli evenly among 4 serving plates. Top each serving with 1/4 of the butter-spice mixture and 1/4 of the soy nuts.

MUSTARD GLAZED BRUSSELS SPROUTS

YIELD: Serves 4

Per portion:

GI: 40
GL: 1.6

CALORIES: 75.5; Carbohydrates: 4g; Fiber: 1.65g; Protein: 1.5g; Fat: 2.75g; Saturated Fat: 1g; Sodium: 149.5mg.

INGREDIENTS:

- 2 cups Brussels sprouts, rinsed and trimmed
- 3/4 cup vegetable broth
- 2 tbsp. Land O Lakes® Spreadable Butter with Canola Oil
- 1 tbsp. Dijon mustard
- 1 tsp. freshly ground black peppercorns

PREPARATION:

1. Rinse Brussels sprouts, cut off tough ends and, if necessary, any outer leaves which do not appear fresh and vital.
2. Place sprouts in a stainless steel colander over a large Dutch oven containing 2 inches of water over medium high heat.
3. Cover and steam Brussels sprouts until tender (about 5-8 minutes). Remove cooked Brussels sprouts to warm serving platter. Cover sprouts to keep warm.
4. Empty the pan, and return the pan to medium heat.
5. Add the vegetable broth, butter, mustard and freshly ground black peppercorns. Whisk the mixture occasionally and simmer for about 2 minutes.
6. Return the Brussels sprouts to the pan, tossing to coat with the sauce.
7. Divide evenly among 4 warm serving plates.

GRANDMA'S SICILIAN SPINACH

YIELD: Serves 2

Per portion:

GI: 40
GL: 3.24

CALORIES: 239.25; Carbohydrates: 8.09g; Fiber: 2.5g; Protein: 7.17g; Fat: 20g; Saturated Fats: 3.5g; Sodium: 184.35mg

INGREDIENTS:

- 2 cups baby spinach leaves, rinsed and drained
- 2 oz. chopped red onion
- 1 oz. daikon radish, rinsed and thinly sliced
- 2 oz. cucumber, peeled, seeded and sliced
- 1 oz. freshly grated ginger root
- 1 extra-large hardboiled egg, sliced
- 1 tbsp. raw sesame seeds
- 1 tbsp. meatless bacon bits

INGREDIENTS FOR DRESSING:

- 2 tbsp. extra virgin olive oil
- 1 tbsp. apple cider vinegar
- 1/2 tbsp. Tamari® Low sodium soy Sauce

PREPARATION:

1. Combine all 3 ingredients for dressing in jar. Cover and shake vigorously.
2. Pour into a chilled salad bowl.
3. Put all salad ingredients on top of dressing in chilled salad bowl. Cover and shake well to combine ingredients.
4. Divide evenly into 2 salad bowls.

BUTTERED SHIRATAKI NOODLES

YIELD: Serves 2

Per portion:

GI: <1
GL: <1

CALORIES: 70; Carbohydrates: 3g; Fiber: 2g; Protein: 1g; Fat: 3.25g; Saturated Fats: 1g; Sodium: 57.5mg

INGREDIENTS:

- One 8 oz. package House Foods Tofu Shirataki Noodle Substitute, immersed into boiling water and drained two times
- 1 tbsp. Land O Lakes® Spreadable Butter with Canola Oil

PREPARATION:

1. Boil two small saucepans of water.
2. Immerse Shirataki noodles in boiling water of first saucepan for 45 seconds, drain.
3. Immerse Shirataki noodles in boiling water of second saucepan for 45 seconds, drain.
4. Mix butter into warm noodles.
5. Divide evenly onto 2 serving plates.

ERNIE'S NOPALITO SALAD ROYALLE

YIELD: Serves 4

Per portion:

GI: 50
GL: 2.17

CALORIES: 96.38; Carbohydrates: 4.33g; Fiber: 2.33g; Protein: 3.05g; Fat: 7.5g; Saturated Fats: 2.25g; Sodium: 47.88mg

INGREDIENTS:

- 1 ¼ cup cooked Nopalito cactus cubes, cooled (Remove thorns first, and then cube cactus and cook cubes, uncovered in boiling water for 15 – 20 minutes.)
- 1 tbsp. finely diced onion
- 1/4 cup diced fresh cilantro
- 1/2 tsp. dried oregano
- 2 tbsp. apple cider vinegar
- 1 tbsp. extra virgin olive oil
- 1/2 cup fresh red ripe tomato slices
- 1/4 cup sliced fresh cilantro
- 1 oz. Monterey Jack cheese, shredded
- 1 tbsp. diced onion
- 1 oz. diced fresh red hot chili pepper (Do not touch with your bear hands.)
- 2 oz. sliced avocado
- 4 outer leaves romaine lettuce, rinsed and dried

PREPARATION:

1. Combine first 6 ingredients in a medium-sized mixing bowl. Cover and refrigerate for 30 minutes.
2. Evenly distribute mixture among 4 salad plates.

3. Top each Nopalito mixture with equal portions of tomato, cilantro, Monterey Jack cheese, onion, red-hot chili pepper, and avocado.
4. Tear romaine leaves in half, and arrange them equally around the sides of each of the 4 salads.

CAULIFLOWER DELIGHT

YIELD: Serves 2

Per portion:

GI: 40
GL: 1.91

CALORIES: 95; Carbohydrates: 4.78g; Fiber: 3.25g; Protein: 2.5g; Fat: 5g; Saturated Fats: 2g; Sodium: 110.4mg

INGREDIENTS:

- 2 cups steamed cauliflower
- 1 tbsp. steamed finely diced onion
- 1 tbsp. steamed finely diced garlic
- 1 oz. fat-free half & half
- 2 tbsp. Land O Lakes® Light Butter with Olive Oil
- 1/4 tsp. freshly ground black peppercorns, to taste
- 1/4 tsp. cayenne pepper, to taste

PREPARATION:

1. Place cauliflower, onion and garlic in a food processor.
2. Pulse on high to form a puree', scraping sides as needed.
3. Add half & half and butter. Pulse on medium a few times to combine.
4. Divide equally onto 2 warm serving plates.
5. Top each serving with a sprinkle of black pepper and cayenne.

BABA GHANOUSH

YIELD: Serves 5

Per portion:

GI: 40
GL: 3.7

CALORIES: 115.75; Carbohydrates: 9.25g; Fiber: 4.4g; Protein: 3g; Fat: 8.2g; Saturated Fats: 1.2g; Sodium: 10.75mg

INGREDIENTS:

- One large eggplant, (yielding 20 oz., cooked according to directions below)
- 2 oz. tahini
- 2 tsp. fresh minced garlic
- 1/4 tsp. cumin
- 1 tbsp. extra virgin olive oil
- 2 oz. freshly squeezed lemon juice
- 1 tbsp. chopped fresh parsley

PREPARATION:

1. Preheat grill or broiler to 400 degrees, and preheat oven to 350 degrees.
2. Pierce eggplant with a fork several times. Place eggplant on grill or broiler rack about 5 inches from heat.
3. Broil or grill for about 15 minutes at 400 degrees, turning occasionally, until skin begins to blacken and blister.
4. Transfer eggplant onto a baking sheet and place in oven at 350 degrees.
5. Bake about 20 minutes, until eggplant becomes soft when pierced with a fork.
6. Remove eggplant from oven or grill; peel off and discard the skin.
7. Place the tender flesh in a mixing bowl.
8. Using an electric hand mixer on low setting, mash the eggplant.

9. In a small mixing bowl, combine the tahini, garlic, lemon juice, and cumin, mixing very well.
10. Add the tahini mixture to the eggplant and combine thoroughly with electric mixer.
11. Distribute equally among 5 serving plates.

CELERY WITH CASHEW BUTTER

YIELD: Serves 1

Per portion:

GI: 25
GL: 2.43

CALORIES: 176; Carbohydrates: 9.72 g; Fiber: 1.6g; Protein: 5.42g; Fat: 14.12g; Saturated Fats: 2.77 g; Sodium: 55 mg

INGREDIENTS:

- 1 twelve inch stalk of organic celery
- 2 tbsp. cashew butter

PREPARATION:

1. Wash, rinse, and dry celery.
2. Spread cashew butter along curve of celery and enjoy.

CELERY WITH HUMMUS

YIELD: Serves 1

Per portion:

GI: 6
GL: .41

CALORIES: 60; Carbohydrates: 6.90 g; Fiber: 2.8g; Protein: 3.32g; Fat: 2.99g; Saturated Fats: .43 g; Sodium: 195 mg

INGREDIENTS:

- 1 twelve inch stalk of organic celery
- 2 tbsp. of commercially prepared hummus

PREPARATION:

1. Wash, rinse, and dry celery.
2. Spread hummus along curve of celery and enjoy.

APPLE SLICES WITH UNSALTED PEANUT BUTTER

YIELD: Serves 1

Per portion:

GI: 38
GL: 8.50

CALORIES: 256; Carbohydrates: 22.58 g; Fiber: 4.8g; Protein: 8.37g; Fat: 16.3g; Saturated Fats: 3.29 g; Sodium: 7 mg

INGREDIENTS:

- 1 medium organic apple (or 120g. apple)
- 2 tbsp. of unsalted organic creamy peanut butter

PREPARATION:

1. Wash, rinse and dry apple.
2. Cut apple in half from the top down.
3. Slice each half into wedges, removing seeds.
4. Place peanut butter in the center of a pretty saucer.
5. Arrange apple slices around peanut butter.

AVOCADO

YIELD: Serves 1

Per portion:

GI: <1
GL: <1

CALORIES: 181; Carbohydrates: 9.64 g; Fiber: 7.6g; Protein: 2.26g; Fat: 16.57g; Saturated Fats: 2.26 g; Sodium: 8 mg

INGREDIENTS:

- 4 oz. (113.39g) of avocado fruit

TOMATO BASIL SOUP

YIELD: Serves 1

Per portion:

GI: 38
GL: 8.36

CALORIES: 100; Carbohydrates: 22 g; Fiber: 2g; Protein: 2.99g; Fat: 0g; Saturated Fats: 0 g; Sodium: 480 mg

INGREDIENTS:

- 1 cup Campbell's Select Harvest Tomato Basil Soup

PREPARATION:

Follow preparation instructions on container.

MINESTRONE SOUP

YIELD: Serves 1

Per portion:

GI: 39
GL: 7

CALORIES: 100; Carbohydrates: 18 g; Fiber: 2.9g; Protein: 5g; Fat: 49g; Saturated Fats: 0 g; Sodium: 480 mg

INGREDIENTS:

- 1 cup Campbell's Select Harvest Minestrone Soup

PREPARATION:

Follow preparation instructions on container.

KIDNEY BEANS

YIELD: Serves 1

Per portion:

GI: 46
GL: 9

CALORIES: 121; Carbohydrates: 21.66 g; Fiber: 7g; Protein: 8.24g; Fat: .48g; Saturated Fats: .10 g; Sodium: 2 mg

INGREDIENTS:

- .95g (about 3 1/3 ounces) dried kidney beans, boiled

PINTO BEANS

YIELD: Serves 1

Per portion:

GI: 39
GL: 9.71

CALORIES: 136; Carbohydrates: 24.91 g; Fiber: 8.5g; Protein: 8.56g; Fat: .62g; Saturated Fats: .30 g; Sodium: 1mg

INGREDIENTS:

- .95g (about 3 1/3 ounces) dried, mature pinto beans, cooked, boiled in water without salt, drained.

LENTIL BEANS

YIELD: Serves 1

Per portion:

GI: 22
GL: 4.20

CALORIES: 110; Carbohydrates: 19.12 g; Fiber: 7.5g; Protein: 8.57g; Fat: .36g; Saturated Fats: .08 g; Sodium: 2 mg

INGREDIENTS:

- .95g (about 3 1/3 ounces) dried green lentil beans, boiled

CANNED PEACHES

YIELD: Serves 1

Per portion:

GI: 52
GL: 9

CALORIES: 53; Carbohydrates: 13g; Fiber: 1.6g; Protein: .75g; Fat: 0g; Saturated Fats: 0g; Sodium: 5mg

INGREDIENTS:

- 120g (4 ¼ ounce) serving Delmonte® (produced in Canada) peaches canned in light syrup

A FRESH PEACH

YIELD: Serves 1

Per portion:

GI: 42
GL: 5

CALORIES: 47; Carbohydrates: 11.45g; Fiber: 1.8g; Protein: 1.09g; Fat: 0g; Saturated Fats: 0g; Sodium: 0mg

INGREDIENTS:

- 1 Beautifully Fresh Peach – organic if possible (120g or 4 ¼ ounces)

A BUNCH OF GRAPES

YIELD: Serves 1

Per portion:

GI: 46
GL: 8

CALORIES: 83; Carbohydrates: 18g; Fiber: 1.1g; Protein: .86g; Fat: 0g; Saturated Fats: 0g; Sodium: 0mg

INGREDIENTS:

- 1 Beautiful small bunch of grapes – organic if possible (120g or 4 ¼ ounces)

A SET OF KIWI FRUIT

YIELD: Serves 1

Per portion:

GI: 47
GL: 6

CALORIES: 73; Carbohydrates: 12g; Fiber: 3.6g; Protein: 1.37g; Fat: .62g; Saturated Fats: .06g; Sodium: 4mg

INGREDIENTS:

- 2 Kiwi fruit, 2 ounces each – organic if possible (120g or 4 ¼ ounces)

A BARTLET PEAR

YIELD: Serves 1

Per portion:

GI: 41
GL: 3

CALORIES: 76; Carbohydrates: 8g; Fiber: 3.7g; Protein: .47g; Fat: .12g; Saturated Fats: .01g; Sodium: 1mg

INGREDIENTS:

- A lovely Bartlett pear – organic if possible (120g or about 4 ¼ ounces)

A COUPLE OF RAW APRICOTS

YIELD: Serves 1

Per portion:

GI: 57
GL: 5

CALORIES: 58; Carbohydrates: 9g; Fiber: 2.4g; Protein: .47g; Fat: .47g; Saturated Fats: g; Sodium: 1mg

INGREDIENTS:

- A couple of perfect apricots – organic if possible (120g or about 4 ¼ ounces)

A FRESH PLUM

YIELD: Serves 1

Per portion:

GI: 24
GL: 3.36

CALORIES: 55; Carbohydrates: 14g; Fiber: 1.7g; Protein: .84g; Fat: 0g; Saturated Fats: 0g; Sodium: 0mg

INGREDIENTS:

- 1 Beautifully Fresh Plum – organic if possible (120g or 4 ¼ ounces)

A FRESH PINK GRAPEFRUIT

YIELD: Serves 1

Per portion:

GI: 25
GL: 3

CALORIES: 38; Carbohydrates: 11g; Fiber: 1.3g; Protein: .76g; Fat: .12g;
Saturated Fats: 0g; Sodium: 0mg

INGREDIENTS:

- 1 Beautifully Fresh Pink Grapefruit – organic if possible (120g or 4 ¼ ounces)

A FRESH ORANGE

YIELD: Serves 1

Per portion:

GI: 42
GL: 3

CALORIES: 59; Carbohydrates: 15g; Fiber: 2.6g; Protein: 1.09g; Fat: 2.6g; Saturated Fats: 0g; Sodium: 1mg

INGREDIENTS:

- 1 Beautifully Fresh orange – organic if possible (120g or 4 ¼ ounces)

KELLOGG'S® ALL-BRAN®

YIELD: Serves 1

Per portion:

GI: 38
GL: 8

CALORIES: 78; Carbohydrates: 21g; Fiber: 8.8g; Protein: 3.94g; Fat: 1.47g; Saturated Fats: .19g; Sodium: 77mg

INGREDIENTS:

- A one ounce serving of Kellogg's® All-Bran manufactured in Battlecreek, Michigan, USA.

WHOLE MILK

YIELD: Serves 1

Per portion:

GI: 41
GL: 5

CALORIES: 149; Carbohydrates: 12g; Fiber: 0g; Protein: 7.69g; Fat: 7.93g; Saturated Fats: 4,51g; Sodium: 105mg

INGREDIENTS:

- 1 cup (8 oz. or about 226g) whole milk, 3.25% milk fat

ALMOND MILK

YIELD: Serves 1

Per portion:

GI: 0
GL: 0

CALORIES: 30; Carbohydrates: 1g; Fiber: 1g; Protein: 1g; Fat: 3g; Saturated Fats: 0g; Sodium: 180mg

INGREDIENTS:

- 1 cup (8 oz. or about 226g) Blue Diamond® Unsweetened Almond Milk

CREAMED COTTAGE CHEESE

YIELD: Serves 1

Per portion:

GI: 30
GL: 1.14

CALORIES: 111; Carbohydrates: 3.82g; Fiber: 0g; Protein: 12.57g; Fat: 4.86g; Saturated Fats: 1.94g; Sodium: 411mg

INGREDIENTS:

- ½ cup (4 oz. or about 226g) creamed cottage cheese

A HARDBOILED EGG

YIELD: Serves 1

Per portion:

GI: <1
GL: <1

CALORIES: 78; Carbohydrates: .56g; Fiber: 0g; Protein: 6.29g; Fat: 5.30g; Saturated Fats: 1.63g; Sodium: 62mg

INGREDIENTS:

- 1 large hardboiled egg, preferably organic free-range omega-3

SARDINES

YIELD: Serves 1

Per portion:

GI: <1
GL: <1

CALORIES: 191; Carbohydrates: 0g; Fiber: 0g; Protein: 10.35g; Fat: 10.53g; Saturated Fats: 1.40g; Sodium: 465mg

INGREDIENTS:

- One 3.75 ounce can Atlantic sardines, packed in oil, drained

A HANDFUL OF MACADAMIA NUTS

YIELD: Serves 1

Per portion:

GI: <1
GL: <1

CALORIES: 204; Carbohydrates: 3.92g; Fiber: 2.4g; Protein: 2.24g; Fat: 21.48g; Saturated Fats: 3.49g; Sodium: 1mg

INGREDIENTS:

- 1 oz. raw macadamia nuts – about 10 to 12 pieces

A HANDFUL OF CASHEWS

YIELD: Serves 1

Per portion:

GI: 25
GL: 2.14

CALORIES: 157; Carbohydrates: 8.56g; Fiber: .9g; Protein: 5.17g; Fat: 12.43g; Saturated Fats: 2.20g; Sodium: 3mg

INGREDIENTS:

- 1 oz. raw cashews – about 10 to 12 pieces

A HANDFUL OF ALMONDS

YIELD: Serves 1

Per portion:

GI: <1
GL: <1

CALORIES: 163; Carbohydrates: 6.14g; Fiber: 3.5g; Protein: 6.09g; Fat: 14.01g; Saturated Fats: 1g; Sodium: 0mg

INGREDIENTS:

- 1 oz. raw almonds – about 10 to 12 pieces

A HANDFUL OF RAW PEANUTS

YIELD: Serves 1

Per portion:

GI: 23
GL: 2

CALORIES: 284; Carbohydrates: 7g; Fiber: 4.2g; Protein: 12.90g; Fat: 24.62g; Saturated Fats: 3.41g; Sodium: 9mg

INGREDIENTS:

- 50g (about 1 3/4 oz.) raw peanuts

A HANDFUL OF PECANS

YIELD: Serves 1

Per portion:

GI: <1
GL: <1

CALORIES: 196; Carbohydrates: 3.93g; Fiber: 2.7g; Protein: 2.60g; Fat: 20.40g; Saturated Fats: 1.75g; Sodium: 0mg

INGREDIENTS:

- 1 oz. raw pecans – about 10 to 12 pieces

A HANDFUL OF WALNUTS

YIELD: Serves 1

Per portion:

GI: 0
GL: 0

CALORIES: 185; Carbohydrates: 3.89g; Fiber: 1.9g; Protein: 4.32g; Fat: 18.49g; Saturated Fats: 1.73g; Sodium: 1mg

INGREDIENTS:

- 1 oz. raw walnuts – about 10 to 12 pieces

YOGURT

YIELD: Serves 1

Per portion:

GI: 18
GL: 3.96

CALORIES: 110; Carbohydrates: 13g; Fiber: 0g; Protein: 1g; Fat: 1g; Saturated Fats: .5g; Sodium: 55mg

INGREDIENTS:

- One four ounce serving Yoplait™ Fat Free Fruit Flavors (various flavors)

SNICKERS® MARATHON ENERGY BAR
CHEWY CHOCOLATE PEANUT BUTTER

YIELD: Serves 1

Per portion:

GI: 36
GL: 9

CALORIES: 210; Carbohydrates: 25g; Fiber: 4g; Protein: 14g; Fat: 7g; Saturated Fats: 3g; Sodium: 240mg

INGREDIENTS:

- One 50g. Bar

SNICKERS® MARATHON LOW CARB LIFESTYLE ENERGY BAR PEANUT BUTTER

YIELD: Serves 1

Per portion:

GI: 21
GL: 2

CALORIES: 210; Carbohydrates: 10g; Fiber: 8g; Protein: 18g; Fat: 5g; Saturated Fats: 2g; Sodium: 180mg

INGREDIENTS:

- One 50g. Bar

SNICKERS® MARATHON NUTRITION BAR

HONEY AND ALMOND

(M&M/MARS, USA)

YIELD: Serves 1

Per portion:

GI: 41
GL: 4

CALORIES: 150; Carbohydrates: 22g; Fiber: 7g; Protein: 10g; Fat: 4.5g; Saturated Fats: 2g; Sodium: 125mg

INGREDIENTS:

- One 50g. Bar

APPENDIX A

Voyage of Discovery: Learning to Build Your Own Low Glycemic Load Recipes

Welcome to our dining table. We hope you have been enjoying the low glycemic load recipes that we have prepared for you. Perhaps you would like to create some of your own.

When you have finished this portion of the book, you will have an understanding of how you can custom build your own *low glycemic load* recipes and meals.

You can begin to create your own unique, *low glycemic load* recipes by using the guidelines provided below and maybe trying out some of the *low GL* foods used in this book or other *low GL* foods you may discover in the references we provide along the way.

A Step-by-Step Adventure in Discovering a New Way of Preparing Meals

To demonstrate the recipe creation process and detail step-by-step how it works, we invite you to join us as we build an authentic low GL roast turkey dinner menu for you and 7 guests. It is more complex than building a single recipe, but through the examples and ideas presented, we believe you will gain an understanding and a creative feel for how it works to build a low GL meal.

For illustration purposes, we'll assume your prospective menu plan includes roast turkey, two green vegetable side dishes, sweet potato, and cranberry sauce, with pumpkin pie for dessert.

Step One: Determining the GI rankings of Foods You Will Use

The first step of creating a *low GL* recipe or meal is to determine the Glycemic Index (GI) rankings of the carbohydrate foods you plan to include in your menu.

The GI represents the quality/potential of a carbohydrate to raise blood glucose levels. The Glycemic Index provides a general estimate of how high and how fast a particular type of carbohydrate is known to raise blood glucose levels. You can interpret the GI ranking by the following scale:

Table A1: The Glycemic Index Ranges from Low to High

Low: 0 - 55
Medium: 56-69
High: 70 +

Resources to Determine the Glycemic Index Rankings of Specific Foods

We are aware of three main resources for glycemic ranking information. Each of the three resources contains a collection of research results from tests conducted throughout the world.

The first two resources are *The International Tables of Glycemic Index and Glycemic Load Values 2008* available online in PDF file format which you can download to your computer. That title refers to two online tables first published in 2008 by the prestigious medical journal Diabetes Care that contain information on 2,480 foods. Those tables are made available by the U.S. National Center for Biotechnology Information which is part of the National Institutes of Health.

That website URL address is:

http://www.ncbi.nlm.nih.gov/pmc/articles/
PMC2584181/bin/dc08-1239_index.html

That URL brings you to a page with hotlinks to two tables and a list of references in PDF format. The first hotlink takes you to Table 1A which contains results on 1,789 carbohydrate-containing foods tested on individuals with normal glucose tolerance. The second hotlink takes you to Table 1B which has only has 608 data entries derived from individuals with impaired glucose tolerance (IGT) and from tests with small subject numbers or values showing wide variability. Still, Table 1B might be useful if you are cooking for someone with IGT.

Once you download and open the tables, Ctrl + F will bring up a little search box where you can enter the names of the carbohydrate-containing foods you want to find the glycemic index ranking for. The left hand column of the chart identifies the food and the next column to the right lists the GI. Most of the entries also have the GL for a specific amount of carbohydrate food on the right hand side of the page. However, if your single serving size contains more or fewer grams of carbohydrate you can do a simple calculation to determine the GL. We will show you how to do that calculation in Step Two.

We introduce you to these tables first because, after downloading them to your computer, you can access the information in these files even when you are not online. They are easy to use since they allow you to review test result details of many foods at the same time. This allows easier planning for a complex meal such as the roast turkey dinner.

The third resource for locating glycemic index rankings is available on an interactive online website located at:

www.Glycemicindex.com

The University of Sydney, in Sydney, Australia, has maintained and updated this resource since 2003.

Determining the Glycemic Index of Your Recipe or Meal

To determine the GI for your recipe or meal, locate the GI ranking of the carbohydrate-containing ingredient or food with the highest GI ranking. This becomes the GI ranking for your entire recipe or meal.

While you are looking at the PDF tables, you might find it convenient to locate the serving sizes and number of carb grams for all of the carbohydrate containing foods in your menu. You need to keep track of the grams of carbohydrate and serving sizes of each food in the meals' menu to determine the GL.

What to do if a Carb Food is Not Listed

Scientists and researchers who compiled the extensive glycemic index data suggest that when a carbohydrate-containing food is unlisted, a specific value could be assigned to that group of foods.

For unlisted dairy products, the assigned value is 30.
In the case of vegetables, the assigned value is 40.

In the case of unlisted fruit, authorities agree that berries are low glycemic because of their high water and fiber content, so they have little glycemic impact. However, since they do have some quantifiable glycemic impact, we have arbitrarily assigned a GI ranking of 50, which is below 55 (low glycemic) and midway on the GI scale of 1 to 100.

You won't find any glycemic index test results for eggs, fish, meat, and poultry (because those high protein foods are not carbohydrate-based), or for avocados (composed mostly of healthy fats), and most salad vegetables because they contain high amounts of fiber and water rather than carbohydrate.

Step Two: Determining the GL

The term *glycemic impact* has to do with the ability of specific amounts of carbo-hydrate to raise blood glucose levels (GI). The Glycemic Load (GL) score quantifies and reveals the glycemic impact of a specific amount of carbohydrate in a single serving of your recipe. You can determine the GL by using a simple formula.

The simple formula looks like this:
GI {Glycemic Index ranking} multiplied by {carb grams} / {divided by} 100 = GL {Glycemic Load score}

Here's an example of how to calculate the GL of a single food, in this case a raw, medium sized Golden Delicious (120g) apple:

First, we find the *Glycemic Index* ranking of the apple in our PDF or online resources. All listings agree that a typical 120 gram serving of Golden Delicious apple contains 16 grams of carbohydrate with a GI rank of 40. To determine its' GL, multiply 40 (the GI ranking) times 16 (the number of carb grams). The result is 640. Then divide 640 by 100, and our final result is 6.4, the GL of that serving of fruit. Since 6.4 is less than 10, this 120 gram apple with 16 grams of carbohydrate has a GL that is considered low glycemic.

In the case of our Golden Delicious apple, here is the formula again with the numbers plugged in:

$$40 \{GI\} \times 16 \{g\ carbs\} = 640 / 100 = 6.4\ GL\ \{GL\ score\}$$

While it is relatively simple to find the GL of a single food item, it's just a little bit trickier to find the GL of a recipe or an entire meal containing several carbohydrate foods.

Determining the GL of a Recipe with Several Carb Sources

To determine the GL for a recipe or meal that contains several sources of carbohydrate, you use the GI score of the ingredient with the highest GI ranking. Then you look up the number of grams of carbohydrate per serving for each carbohydrate containing ingredient in your recipe or menu. Now you total all the grams of carbohydrate.

Next, you multiply the total grams of carbohydrate by the GI score of the carbohydrate ingredient with the highest GI ranking.

After you multiply, divide that result by 100. Now you have the GL score for your recipe or meal. The formula:

GI {Glycemic Index ranking of carb source with highest GI} X {multiplied by total carbs per serving} / {divided by} 100 = GL {Glycemic Load score}

You can interpret the GL score by the following scale:

Table A2

Low Glycemic Load: 0 – 10
Medium Glycemic Load: 11 -19
High Glycemic Load: 20 +

When building a recipe for a specific number of servings, you might find it easier to work with the total carbs in the entire recipe. In this case, you add up all the grams of carbohydrate and divide that total by the number of servings your recipe will provide to give you the number of carbs per serving. Now use your carbs per serving number to multiply by the highest GI ingredient in your recipe when you figure the GL.

Step Three: Gathering the Rest of the Nutrition Facts

When building new low GL recipes from scratch, you need to know the amount of carbohydrate, but you may also want to know the amount of calories, protein, sodium, saturated fat, and fiber your recipe will provide. A very helpful resource for those nutrient contents of foods is the *USDA National Nutrient Database for Standard Reference* at: http://ndb.nal.usda.gov/.

That easy-to-use interactive online resource provides information on a broad scope of nutrition data including some mineral, vitamin, and lipid content of the ingredients you are researching for use in your recipes. You can even plug in the exact quantity of the food you want information for to get the number of calories, and the specific amounts of carbohydrate, protein, fat, saturated fat, and milligrams of sodium, calcium, potassium, magnesium or other nutrients relevant to your recipe planning.

A second excellent source is *The Diabetes Carbohydrate and Fat Gram Guide* by Lea Ann Holzmeister, RD, CDE published by the *American Diabetes Association* and *the American Dietetic Association* in 2000. Now on its 4th Edition (September, 2010), this handy 725 page guide now includes an index. Here you will find more than carbohydrate and fat measurements, but also the number of calories, and the amounts of saturated fats, cholesterol, sodium, fiber, and protein in common North American foods, including some "convenience foods" and "fast foods."

Still another excellent resource is the book *Nutrition Almanac* by John D. Kirschmann published in 2007 by Nutrition Search, Inc. This book, originally published in 1976 is now in its 7th printed edition. Within its covers you will find information on not only basic nutrition facts of foods such as those covered in the USDA Database and the *Carbohydrate and Fat Gram Guide*, but also more in-depth coverage of the vitamin, mineral and amino acid content of basic foods. (There are 9 essential amino acids which we must get from the food we eat, that is why we call them "essential." The foods that contain all 9 essential amino acids are eggs, fish, meat, dairy products, poultry, seafood, and soy protein.)

Another method is to look at the labels on any packaged foods you may choose to buy. The Nutrition Facts box provides information on calories, fat, saturated fat, sodium, and protein amounts plus the crucial number of carbohydrate grams per serving. You will use the "amount per serving" and the portion size as you calculate the *Glycemic Load* of whatever recipe or meal you are creating.

Now, Back to Your Menu

Green Vegetables

Vegetables are carbohydrate-containing foods and all carbs count when you calculate the glycemic load of a recipe or meal. Most vegetables carry an assigned GI of 40. Using an assigned value (unless another carb ingredient has a higher GI) gives you a GI number with which to multiply the total number of carbohydrate grams in a serving of your meal to determine the glycemic load.

Perhaps you decide that you'd like to sample a couple of vegetable side dish recipes you reviewed in this book. Maybe the Tangy Tomato & Cucumber Salad sounds good to you, and you think that would be a tasty addition to your menu. You can find the recipe in our table of contents. From the recipe, you learn that a 113g (4 oz.) serving has 2.75g carbs. But you decide a 56g (2 oz.) serving will be just the right amount for you. That reduces the carb portion of the serving to just 1.38g carbs.

The gently steamed Parisian Asparagus recipe in this book would bring a nice fresh green vegetable to your plate and add only 2g carbs from its'113g (4 oz.) serving. However, your "just right" amount is a 56g (2 oz.) serving. That reduces the carb content of the asparagus to one carb gram.

Sweet Potato

The 2008 Edition of Tables of GL does not have a listing for any sweet potatoes grown in the USA or North America, but they do report that 70 is the "mean of 9 studies" for sweet potatoes grown in other countries. You know that 70 is high glycemic. The 2008 Tables of GL also inform us that there are 22 of carbohydrate in a 150g serving, with a GL of 22. That's definitely a high glycemic load so sweet potatoes are not welcome with this turkey dinner.

What about changing the menu and substituting mashed potatoes and gravy? The first step is to look up the GI of potatoes in our resources. If you are considering instant mashed potatoes, you find the Idahoan brand, from Lewisville, Idaho has a GI of 87. That's even higher than the sweet potato. You also note that there are 20g of carbohydrate within a 150g serving, with a GL of 17.40. Those numbers indicate that that serving would deliver a medium glycemic load.

How about using regular whole potatoes instead of instant mashed potatoes? Look at the *2008 Tables* again. The USA Baked Russet has a GI of 94 (that's almost as high as pure glucose at 100). The USA Russet has 30 g of carbs in a 150 gram serving. This spud delivers a GL of 28. According to those Tables, even the potatoes grown in other countries are too high glycemic to use.

Tasty alternative for mash potatoes

What about considering a substitute faux potato recipe custom built just for this purpose? With our *Cauliflower Delight* recipe, you can eat just over 226g (a whole cup) containing only 4.78g of carbs, according to the *USDA* Database. With a GI of 40, the glycemic load is only 1.91 for that one cup serving. Finely mashed cauliflower topped with gravy actually tastes like mashed potatoes and gravy. Furthermore, 113g (about 4 oz.) contains only 2.39 grams of carbohydrate while still providing a satisfying serving size. In addition, this smaller amount of carbohydrate leaves plenty of room for other carbohydrates in the remainder of your meal.

Cranberry Sauce

You will find no listing for cranberry sauce among our glycemic index resources. In the case of unlisted fruits, the specific GI value assigned is 50.

Your investigation continues when you are at the supermarket and you pick up a can of jellied cranberry sauce and look at the Nutrition Box to find out how many carbohydrate grams are in a serving. You discover that a 56g (2 oz.) serving has 25g of carbohydrates (of which 21g are empty calories from added sugar.) You pick up another brand and discover it has the same amount of carb and sugar grams. The assigned GI of 50 for the cranberries with 25g of carbs for the 56g serving gives you a GL of 12.50 so those brands of cranberry sauce would deliver a medium glycemic load.

That's not good enough for our goal of creating a complete low glycemic load meal so we then look up plain cranberries in the *USDA Nutrient Database.* We learn that a 56g (2 oz.) serving has only 3g of carbs. Consequently you realize that you could make your own cranberry sauce and eliminate those 21g of sugar carbs (which carry a high GI ranking of 60) found in the store brands of cranberries.

You know that natural cranberries aren't very sweet so decide to add a low glycemic sweetener. Coconut Palm sugar has a GI ranking of only 35. This unrefined sweetener has naturally occurring nutrients including amino acids, B vitamins, iron, magnesium, potassium, and zinc. A tbsp. of coconut palm sugar has 12g carbs, compared to 9g carbs in the same amount of table sugar. However, the lower GI ranking of the coconut sugar creates a GL score of 4.2 for a tablespoon of coconut sugar.

Liquid Stevia drops are another natural sweetening option you can use instead of sugar – without adding any calories or any extra carbs to your cranberry sauce. (If you use the packet variety of stevia, the fillers added to each packet of the product add 1g of carbohydrate to your recipe.) If you want to add a little extra flavor, you might like to add a tbsp. of some freshly grated orange rind to the water as you simmer your whole berries. For our example, we'll use liquid stevia. (The whole house smells great as this combination simmers!)

Pumpkin Pie
In the past, you perhaps selected a commercially prepared pumpkin pie for dessert. However, with your new found low GL knowledge you suspect such a pie would carry a high GL. You determine that your suspicion is correct when you check the glycemic index resources and find the only low glycemic pumpkin listed is the Butternut pumpkin from Australia. This particular variety of pumpkin has a GI of 51 with 6g of carbs in an 80g serving, giving it a GL of 3.

Since we have a potential GI of 51 for the pumpkin, you look up the number of carbs for your customary commercially prepared pumpkin pie in our *USDA Nutrient Database*. You learn that an 80g serving (just under 3 ounces) of commercially prepared pumpkin pie delivers almost 28 grams of carbohydrates. You do the math and discover that just that one commercially prepared slice of pie has a GL of over 14. Where did all those carbs come from? Nearly 20% of that pie slice is sugar.

Out of curiosity, you do a little search to learn more about the Butternut pumpkin. You find Butternut pumpkin in Australia to be what we call Butternut squash in the USA, and readily available as commercially canned pumpkin.

So you look up canned pumpkin on the *USDA Nutrient Database* to find that there are 6.47g of carbs in an 80g (just under 3 oz.) serving. The GL of that serving of pumpkin is 3.30.

The next step to creating a great low GL pumpkin pie is to consider how to make its' crust. You *can't* make it with white flour because when you look up white flour on the GI tables you find that the "mean (average of test results) of 16 studies" for white flour is a GI of 70. With 15g of carbs in a 30g (1 oz.) serving, this would give your slice of pie, including the custard filling, a GL over 15, quite a bit above the low GL cut-off of 10. Fixated on delivering a complete low glycemic load meal, you would decide that no matter how you slice it, you would rather not eat that particular slice of pie.

Alternative Pumpkin Pie
How about if you made pumpkin custard for dessert instead of a pie? Isn't the custard the best part of the pie, anyway? You could use stevia for sweetening instead of sugar, and add the seasonings you like best. We will use liquid stevia again for our example.

We're almost there. You didn't realize that it could take so much work to develop a low glycemic load meal from scratch did you?

Aren't you glad that in this book you have 120 authentic, low GL recipes already created and waiting for you? The recipes can give you a superb start on eating low GL foods. Once you become more familiar with the foods and food combinations that will work best for you, you will find it a lot easier to create your own low GL recipes and meals.

But wait: What about some gravy for those "mashed potatoes?"

Gravy
You really love to make your own gravy from scratch. You know there are no carbs in the juice from the turkey, so that will not affect the glycemic value of your meal. The carbs come from whatever you use to thicken that juice to turn it into gravy. White, unbleached flour has a GI of 70 and 15g (1 tbsp.) has 5.72g of carbs. If you used that tablespoon of white flour, the GI of 70 for the gravy would be the highest GI number in your meal. If you went with the flour, the GL for the 14.88g carbs in your meal would be 10.41, no longer low GL. That is due to the impact of the GI of 70 for the flour. As an alternative, you could

substitute a lower carb thickener for the high GI flour. One thickening option would be to use soy lecithin granules, a lipid that would also thicken your gravy adding only 1g carb for 15g (1 tbsp.) compared to the 5.72g carbs in the same amount of white flour.

By substituting the soy lecithin granules for the white flour, the butternut pumpkin, with a GI of 51, will be the highest GI in your meal. This is the number we use when we multiply by the total number of carbohydrate grams in your meal to determine the glycemic load.

If you decide you will enjoy an ounce of gravy thickened with soy lecithin, here are the serving sizes, carb counts and the glycemic load for your entire meal:

Complete Carb Count for Roast Turkey Dinner

Recipe	Serving Size	Carbs
Tangy Tomato & Cucumber Salad	56g (2 oz.)	1.38g
Parisian Asparagus	56g (2 oz.)	1g
Cauliflower Delight (mashed potato substitute)	113g (4 oz.)	2.9g
Cranberry Sauce	56g (2 oz.)	3g
Pumpkin Pie (custard)	80g (3 oz.)	6.47g
Gravy thickened with soy lecithin granules	28g (1 oz.)	0.13g
Total	389g (14 oz.)	14.88g

So far your total meal carb content is only 14.88 grams. Multiply that amount by the GI ranking for the highest carbohydrate ingredient (51) and you get 758.88. Divide by 100 to arrive at the glycemic load of 7.59. Now you have the GL score for your meal. It is under10 so it is a low glycemic load meal. Here is the formula with the numbers plugged in:

51 {GI} X 14.88 {g carbs} = 758.88 / {divided by} 100 = 7.59 {GL}

These calculations prove that your meal is truly a low glycemic load meal.

Your Body is the Greatest Miracle in the World

Whatever you can do to come closer to these hypothetical numbers will improve your health. Just finding this new information on some of the best low GL foods to eat is a great beginning to enhancing your health.

Life is life and numbers are only numbers. Be gentle with yourself and take time to enjoy each step along the way. As you incorporate changes into your meal planning and preparation, take it one step at a time. Each step is a step in the right direction.

Spend some thoughtful moments several times each day appreciating the marvelous creation that is your body. Perhaps while you are taking a walk or doing some stretching is a good time for you to focus inward with love. Have faith in your body's inborn capacity for healing and rejuvenation.

Consider that during every second of your life, two million of your red blood cells die and are replaced by two million more in a symphony that has taken place since your birth.

Your heart beats about a hundred thousand times a day to pump about two thousand gallons of blood each day through almost sixty thousand miles of arteries, capillaries, and veins to supply every cell in your body with freshly oxygenated blood and the nutrients your body needs.

Your body is the greatest miracle of creation. The quality of the foods you provide for the cells of your body make all the difference. Treat your body well with low GL foods. We know you will enjoy the recipes in this book. They may inspire you to create your own low GL meal recipes. If you do, we encourage you to share them with us. Send them to RecipeCreators@lowglycemichappiness.com.

Judith M Lickus, BS, LBSW
Director, Recipe Division
Diabetes Manager, LLC

APPENDIX B: THE HEART OF THE MATTER

How Low Glycemic Eating Promotes Health and Happiness

A mass of scientific, medical, and nutritional research including the landmark *Nurse's Health Study and the Health Professional Follow-Up Study*[1] have discovered links between *high carbohydrate* intake, as measured by *glycemic load*,[2] and increased risks for the development of type 2 diabetes, cardiovascular diseases (CVDs), and Metabolic Syndrome (MetS) especially in women. MetS is a constellation of disorders including hypertension and high levels of both cholesterol and triglycerides. All three increase the risks of cardiovascular diseases including Coronary Heart Disease.[3]

Indeed, nutritional research has found that both younger and middle-age women who drink large quantities of beverages sweetened by High Fructose Corn Syrup (HFCS) are particularly vulnerable. Experts believe that *high glycemic* HFCSs are a factor in the increase of weight and development of type 2 diabetes in those women.

Another link to diabetes and cardiovascular diseases that research has found are deficits in the intake of healthy dietary omega 3 fatty acids. Both

---

1 Hu FB, Willett WC: **Diet and coronary heart disease: findings from the Nurses' Health Study and Health Professionals' Follow-up Study.** *Journal of Nutritional Health and Aging* 2001, **5:**132-138.

2 Dong JY, Zhang YH, Wang P, Qin LQ. Meta-analysis of dietary glycemic load and glycemic index in relation to risk of coronary heart disease. *American Journal of Cardiology.* 2012; 109:1608–1613; Beulens JW, De Bruijne LM, Stolk RP, Peeters PH, Bots ML, Grobbee DE, et al. High dietary glycemic load and glycemic index increased risk of cardiovascular disease among middle-aged women: a population – based follow-up study. *Journal of the American College of Cardiology.* 2007 July 3;50(1):14-21

3 McKeown NM, Meigs JB, Liu S, Saltzman E, Wilson PW, Jacques PF. Carbohydrate nutrition, insulin resistance, and the prevalence of the metabolic syndrome in the Framingham Offspring Cohort. *Diabetes Care.* 2004. February; 27(2):538-46.

low intake of omega 3 fatty acids and the increased intake of high fructose soft drinks are thought to contribute not only to the development of diabetes, but also MetS and to Non-Alcoholic Fatty Liver disease, according to the experts.[4]

Those research results and plenty of others point to improved well-being provided by avoiding unhealthy *high glycemic* diets. *Low Glycemic Happiness* recipes include only *low glycemic load meals,* all the lowest of the low in terms of carbohydrate (30 grams or less per entree) to assure a *low glycemic impact.*

Health Benefits of *Low GL* Foods

While the intake of *high glycemic foods* seem to attract diseases and disorders like a huge magnet, an equally impressive mass of scientific, medical, and nutritional research indicates that *low glycemic load* meals, such as those used in the recipes of this book, *can help you* avoid cardiovascular diseases such as stroke *and hypertension, and lifestyle diseases such as obesity, depression, and MetS.*

As an example, the authors of the *Framingham, Massachusetts Offspring Study,* which studied over 5,000 volunteers, besides linking high glycemic foods to MetS also pointed out that *low glycemic* foods may be the antidote for MetS and related diseases. The study authors concluded that "Given that both a high cereal fiber content and lower glycemic index are attributes of whole-grain foods, recommendations to increase whole-grain intake may *reduce* the risk of developing the metabolic syndrome."[5]

The list of research studies proclaiming the superiority of *low glycemic* foods keeps growing. Published earlier this year was a systematic review and meta-analysis of several different approaches to the management of type 2 diabetes. The study looked at 20 randomized clinical trials with a total of 3460 subjects to assess the effects of various diets on glycemic control and weight loss. The researchers knew there was plenty of evidence that reducing blood glucose concentrations, inducing weight loss, and improving the lipid profile reduces

---

4 Schulze, MB, Manson JE, Ludwig DS, Colditz GA, Stampfer MJ Willett WC, & Hu, FB. "Sugar-sweetened beverages, weight gain and incidence of type 2 diabetes in young and middle-aged women *JAMA* 2004, 292, 927-934.

5 Ibid: McKeown, Meigs, Liu, Saltzman, Wilson, and Jacques. Carbohydrate nutrition, insulin resistance, and the prevalence of the metabolic syndrome in the Framingham Offspring Cohort. *Diabetes Care.* 2004.

cardiovascular risk in people with type 2 diabetes. However, among those many diets and eating plans they wanted to find out which were the best ways to achieve reduced blood glucose concentrations while losing excess weight. Their *meta-analysis* (a study analyzing the results of many studies) concluded that: "Low carbohydrate, low-GI, Mediterranean and high-protein diets are effective in improving various markers of cardiovascular risks in people with diabetes and should be considered in the overall strategy of diabetes management."[6]

Your Healthy Metabolism is in the BAG

One of the more interesting studies on reversing serious metabolic abnormalities compared a low carb/high protein diet called LoBAG, for "Low Biologically Available Glucose," a longwinded way to say *low glycemic load*. The researchers found that the LoBAG (think *low glycemic load*) diet "dramatically reduced circulating blood glucose levels in people with untreated type 2 diabetes.

"Potentially this could be a patient-empowering way to ameliorate hyperglycemia [the most severe form of diabetes] without pharmacological intervention," wrote the authors of the study.[7]

In other words, cutting out *high glycemic* carbohydrate foods allowed the subjects of that study – even though their diabetes was untreated in any other way – to "dramatically reduce their blood glucose levels" *without the use of anti-diabetes medications.* The only downside of that study was that it was a short-term pilot study including only eight men.

Fortunately, Swedish researchers from the Department of Medicine of Blekingesjukuset Medical Center in Karishamn, Sweden upped the stakes in terms of numbers studied for a longer period of time – six months.

The Swedes studied 31 obese individuals with type 2 diabetes. Sixteen of the subjects were put on a low carbohydrate diet of 1800 calories for men and 1600 for women. Only 20% of those calories were from carbohydrate, 30% was

6 Ajala O, English P, Pinkney J, Systematic review and meta-analysis of different dietary approaches to the management of type 2 diabetes. *American Journal of Clinical Nutrition.* 2013 March, 97(3):505-16. Doi: 10.3945/ajcn.112.042457.

7 Gannon MC, Nuttall FQ. Effect of a high-protein, low-carbohydrate diet on blood glucose control in people with type 2 diabetes. *Diabetes.* 2004. September; 53(9); 2375-82.

protein and 50% was fat. The remaining 15 type 2 individuals were the control group. Those in the control group went on the typical American high carbohydrate diet consisting of 60% carbohydrates, 15% protein, and 25% fat.

Large changes in blood glucose levels were seen almost immediately in the low carb group. After six months "a marked reduction in bodyweight of patients in the low carbohydrate diet group was observed and this remained one year later" stated the researchers in an abstract to their work that was published in *Ups Journal of Medical Science* in Sweden.

The Swedish researchers concluded: "A low carbohydrate diet is an effective tool in the treatment of obese patients with type 2 diabetes."[8]

Regardless of the carbohydrate source, at least 90% of all carb grams convert to glucose in the bloodstream. However, in comparison to high glycemic load foods, low glycemic load carbohydrates convert to glucose slowly.

After a high glycemic meal, blood sugar levels jump for both healthy people and for those with diabetes or prediabetes (also known as Impaired Glucose Tolerance, IGT).

> Within one hour after eating a high glycemic meal, the blood sugar levels of people with normal glucose tolerance start to plunge because their pancreas rapidly makes enough insulin to convert the glucose into energy – or store it as fat.

As a result, their blood sugar levels quickly tumble and many people reach for another high-carb, high-glycemic snack, igniting yet another sugar spike explosion skyrocketing their blood sugar levels higher again. Skyrocketing blood sugars are once again followed by plunges. That's why the peaks and valleys of blood sugar levels are likened to riding a roller coaster and even those with normal glucose tolerance may start to feel tired and cranky when they arrive at those low blood sugar levels after a high glycemic load meal. After a high

---

8 Nielsen JV, Jonsson E, Nilsson AK. Lasting improvement of hyperglycemia (standard British spelling for this disorder) and bodyweight: low carbohydrate diet in type 2 diabetes. A brief report. *Ups Journal of Medical Science.* 2005;110(2):179-83.

glycemic load meal, a person with normal glucose tolerance may have a blood sugar level surge to about 180 mg per dl and then plunge to their normal range somewhere between 80-120 mg/per dl. Some may even notice that their level is lower than it was before the high glycemic meal.

On the other hand, after a high glycemic load meal, the blood sugar levels of people with IGT or full diabetes remain high longer. That's why people with type 2 diabetes who are on insulin are encouraged to check their blood sugars with a glucose meter about 2 hours after a meal.

For those with diabetes or IGT, it's not unusual for high glycemic load meals to cause blood glucose levels to soar past 200 to 230, 250 or even higher! If on insulin, their next step is to take a shot of fast-acting insulin to lower their blood glucose to normal levels. If not on insulin, some people with diabetes or IGT can bring their sugars down with as little as 30 minutes of exercise. Brisk walking often does the trick. They are also advised not to add to their already high glucose levels when it comes time for another meal!

Much better food choices for everyone, regardless of glucose tolerance levels, involve choosing food sources with good amounts of protein, healthy fats, and fiber. Those factors go hand-in-hand with *low glycemic load* eating. Those ingredients trigger lower glycemic responses followed by a gentle decline in blood glucose levels. Incidentally, that keeps you feeling full and satisfied for longer periods of time.

Please realize that the *Low Glycemic Happiness Collection* recipes presented in this book aren't *just* another low carbohydrate eating plan. Even though the contents of the recipes here are, indeed, low carbohydrate – 30 grams or less per entrée; they are also *low glycemic* as defined by their *Glycemic Load (GL).*

Our recipes provide both *low glycemic* and *low carbohydrate* food choices in amounts that will not only satisfy your appetite, but they will help you maintain stable blood glucose levels.

Protect Yourself from Metabolic Syndrome (MetS)

It is well known that Metabolic Syndrome (MetS) has been called a global epidemic by the World Health Organization (WHO)[9] and is considered to be a major public health problem, with 34% of all Americans over the age of 20 estimated to be affected[10]. What is less well known is that the MetS global epidemic "is one of the few clinical syndromes that affect a large portion of the general population that is potentially reversible by established interventions.[11] The authors of this study postulate that "insulin resistance-associated impairment in cerebrovascular reactivity is an important mechanism underlying brain deficits seen in MetS[12] that can lead to Alzheimer's and Parkinson's diseases.

The "established interventions" effective against MetS that the authors referred to include weight loss[13] and pharmacological interventions. Both of those interventions reduce *insulin resistance*. Another effective food-oriented intervention is Fish Oils rich in omega-3 fatty acids. Artemis P. Simopoulos of the *Center for Genetics, Nutrition and Health* states that, "Fish oil supplementation maintains proper insulin signaling in the brain, ameliorates Non Alcoholic Fatty Liver Disease and decreases the risk to metabolic syndrome suggesting that adequate levels of omega-3 fatty acids in the diet can cope with the metabolic challenges imposed by high fructose intake in Western diets.[14]

9   Poenza MV, Mechanick JI. The metabolic syndrome: definition, global impact, and pathophysiology. *Nutritional Clinical Practice*. 2009;24:560-577.

10   Ervin RB. Prevalence of metabolic syndrome among adults 20 years of age and over, by sex, age, race, and ethnicity, and body mass index: United States, 2003-2006. *National Health Statistics Report*. 2009;13:1-7.

11   Yates, KF, Sweat V, Po Lai Yau, Turchiano, MM Convit A. Impact of Metabolic Syndrome on Cognition and Brain: A selected review of the literature. *Arteriosclerosis, Thrombosis, and Vascular Biology*. 2012;32:2060-2067. Online edition doi: 10.1161/ATVBAHA.112.252759.

12   Ibid Yates.

13   Case CC, Jones PH, Nelson K, O'Brian Smith E, Gallantyne CM. Impact of weight loss on the metabolic syndrome. *Diabetes Obesity Metabolism*.2002, November; 4(6):407-414.

14   Simopoulos AP. Dietary Omega-3 Fatty Acid Deficiency and High Fructose intake in the development of Metabolic Syndrome, brain metabolic abnormalities, and Non-Alcoholic Fatty Liver Disease. *Nutrients*, 2013 January;5(8):2901-2923. Doi: 10.3390/nu5082901

> Which would you rather use to protect yourself: Prescription drugs that may have side effects and risk interactions with other drugs or our *Low Glycemic Happiness* recipes which feature plenty of Omega-3 carrying fish meals?

That Great Mood You Ordered Is Coming Right Up

Protect Yourself against Bad Moods

An interesting study was conducted on mood and cognitive response using 42 healthy overweight volunteers, all about 35 (+ or – 5) years of age. Researchers studied the long term effects of energy restricted low glycemic load (LGL) diets and high glycemic load (HGL) diets by providing the 42 subjects all food, caloric beverages, and a multivitamin supplements for a 6 month period.

Since the researchers controlled the types and amounts of food provided to the volunteers, the results of this highly controlled dietary intake provide a unique lens through which to trace the emergence of happy or sad (depressed) emotions. Indeed, the results indicated that LGL eating patterns...

"Protect against negative moods which occur during weight loss when a conventional HG diet is consumed," wrote the authors of the study.

"Additionally," they continued, "Our results lend support to accumulating evidence of broadly beneficial health effects of low GL diets compared to HG diets in weight management."[15]

Those "beneficial health effects" include reversal of hypertension, stabilized blood glucose levels, and normalized lipid levels in the bloodstream.

---

15 Cheatam RA., Roberts S., Sai Krupa Das; Gilhooly CH., Golden, JK., Hyatt, R et al. "Long-term effects of provided low and high glycemic load & low energy diet on mood and cognition" *Physiological Behaviour*, 2009 September 7;98(3):374-379. DOI: 10.1016/j.physbeh.2009.06.015.

A Secret of Happiness – *The Essential Amino Acids*

Diets high in carbohydrate but low in fat and protein sometimes do not provide all nine *essential amino acids* necessary for good health. On the other hand, *Low Glycemic Happiness* foods – such as such as eggs, fish, meat, dairy products, poultry, seafood, and soy protein – provide adequate amounts of protein containing all 9 essential amino acids. Consequently, your low GL low carb breakfast is a great way to begin your morning! Aren't you glad our *Low Glycemic Happiness Recipes* are based on a wide variety of food sources containing all nine of the *Essential Amino Acids*? That's another reason for happiness.

###

APPENDIX C: BRIEF HISTORY OF GLYCEMIC IMPACT RESEARCH

In the 1980's and well into the 1990's, carbohydrate foods were classified as simple or complex based on the number of simple sugars in the carbohydrate molecule of the food being considered. Carbohydrates such fructose or sucrose (table sugar, which is composed of one molecule of glucose and one of fructose) were considered "simple" while starchy foods were labeled "complex" because starch is composed of long chains of simple sugars (glucose and fructose).

Consequently, dietary advice to people with diabetes before and during that period consisted of "eat less simple and more complex carbohydrates." That wrongheaded advice was given on the assumption that consuming starchy foods would lead to small increases in blood glucose levels.

The assumption was wrong.

In 1981, Dr. Thomas Wolever and Dr. David Jenkins at the University of Toronto proposed the initial concept of a *Glycemic Index* for all carbohydrate-containing foods. Their glycemic index concept was thought to be a helpful boon to individuals with diabetes in the control of their blood glucose levels. It took over a decade for science to realize that the Glycemic Load is the other half of the calculation that actually measures the glycemic load impact of foods.

To determine the glycemic impact of individual carbohydrate-containing foods, in a landmark study the University of Toronto researchers recruited panels of 8-10 volunteers to test each of several hundred carbohydrate foods. After an overnight fast, blood samples were taken from volunteers who then were provided with a serving of a test food containing approximately 50 grams of digestible carbohydrate. Then, the researchers measured and recorded the changes in the volunteer's blood sugar levels every 15 minutes during a 2-hour period. On a separate occasion, as a comparison or reference control, the same volunteers for the tested food, after another overnight fast, were given a 50g carb portion of *straight glucose* to determine its' impact on the blood sugar levels of the volunteers' during a similar 2 hour test period. The 15 minute intervals of both tests were graphed to determine the Area under the Curve (AUC) of both tests.

To determine the tested food's rank on the *Glycemic Index,* the area under the curve is divided by the corresponding area under the curve when a reference food – usually glucose and/or bread – is eaten. The result of that division indicates a ranking on the *Glycemic Index* somewhere between 0 and 100. Pure Glucose is ranked at 100. Any carbohydrate containing food ranked 55 or under is considered low glycemic – 80 to 100 is high glycemic.

It wasn't until 1997, that Harvard professors led by Dr. Walter Willett introduced the *Glycemic Load* to account for the quantity of a carbohydrate serving, in other words the old-fashioned concept of portion control reintroduced. About time! The *Glycemic Load* is a dietary index that measures the power of specific amounts of carbohydrate to raise human blood glucose levels. The *Glycemic Index (GI)* ranking and the total number of carbohydrates are both necessary to determine a *Glycemic Load (GL)* score. Therefore, the GL considers portion sizes, the impact from the actual amount of carbohydrate that you eat at any one time.

The GI established new accuracy in the measurement of a carbohydrate-containing foods' impact.

In fact, today the *Glycemic Load* is the accepted and most accurate predictor of our bodies' response to the glycemic impact of a carbohydrate-based food.

Over the years, researchers around the world, using methodology pioneered by Wolever and Jenkins, replicated the Toronto study using other sources of carbohydrate foods grown in their own countries. The glycemic index data derived from those studies were published in peer-reviewed medical and nutrition journals and later on the *Glycemic Index* website established in 2002 by the University of Sydney, Sydney, Australia.

Why Should You Care About This?

You should care about these facts because *low glycemic* eating, specifically *Low Glycemic Load* (LGL) eating (which allows you to factor in the *amount* of carbohydrate ingested) *is healthier for you.*

On one hand, HGL foods increase blood sugar levels rapidly and higher than LGL foods. The rapid increases in blood glucose signal beta cells on the pancreas to increase the secretion of insulin. High insulin levels can result in sharp decreases in blood glucose and can lead to hypoglycemia (dangerously low blood glucose levels) which, in turn, can cause you to reach for more high glycemic foods to send blood glucose to new heights.

These rapid blood glucose swings over time can burn out pancreatic beta cells and lead to diabetes or even cause hyperglycemia, the most severe form of type 2 diabetes.

A Limitation of the Glycemic Index

The *Glycemic Index,* while an amazing example of collaborative research over the years, had one great limitation. It didn't take into account the quantity or amount of carb content eaten. To accurately determine GI scale rankings while serving sizes varied, the amount of the foods tested almost always contained 50 grams of carbohydrate. That's because standardized testing would result in a true Glycemic Index scale. Since Wolever and Jenkins tested 50 grams of carbohydrate in various portion sizes of the tested food in their landmark study, 50 grams, with few exceptions, became the de facto standard used to determine the glycemic impact of the carbohydrate test food.

The serving size of the food being tested didn't matter as long as the serving size contained within it 50 grams of carbohydrate. To put into perspective the reason why most vegetables are low glycemic, realize that it takes 8 cups of chopped broccoli to provide 50 grams of actual carbohydrate. On the other hand, 50 g of carbs is contained in only 3 1/3 tbsp. of glucose. No wonder glucose is rated at 100 on the Glycemic Index.

In the real world we commonly eat serving sizes that contain various amounts of carbohydrate, sometimes higher and sometimes lower than the standardized 50 grams used to determine the GI. Let's go back to that Golden Delicious apple mentioned in Appendix A. Remember that apple contained 16 grams of carbohydrate within its' total 120 gram serving weight. The GI ranking for apple is 40 so 40 times 16 grams divided by 100 = 6.4. Since 6.4 is below the boundary of 10 between low and medium glycemic foods, the medium-sized 120 gram apple carries a low glycemic load.

But what if we wanted to eat a larger apple, a huge Golden Delicious apple weighting 240 grams? Since the huge Golden Delicious is twice the weight of the smaller apple, we can guess that it contains a higher amount of carbohydrate grams which, of course, would have a larger glycemic impact, but we don't want to guess.

To the Rescue, the Glycemic Load

The benefit of figuring the glycemic load of a carbohydrate-containing food serving is that it measures the glycemic impact of that *particular serving size*.

The GL of a food is determined by multiplying its' GI ranking by the total amount of carb grams in a single serving of the food. The apple's GI ranking of 40 remains the same but the 32 grams of carbs included in the bigger apple (twice the amount of carbohydrate of the smaller apple) times 40 = 1240 divided by 100 = 12.8. That's above the LGL top boundary of 10 so the larger 240 g. apple containing 32 g of carbohydrate is not *low glycemic*. Serving size does matter.

Back to the Glycemic Impact Timeline

Between 1981 and 1995, researchers around the world, using the methodology pioneered by Wolever and Jenkins, replicated the Toronto study using other sources of carbohydrate foods grown in their own countries. The glycemic index data derived from those studies were published in peer-reviewed medical and nutrition journals.

In 1995 all that information (565 separate entries) was consolidated by Kaye Foster Powell and Janette Brand-Miller and published as a paid supplement in the *American Journal of Clinical Nutrition* as a scale, suggested and initially demonstrated by Wolever and Jenkins in 1981, which is now known as the *International Tables of Glycemic Index*. (Sponsors included the Australian Sugar Industry, the Australian branch of the Kellogg cereal company, Goodmen Fielder Ltd, Mead Johnson Nutritional Group and the Ricegrowers Cooperative, Ltd.)

Worldwide research persisted on other carbohydrate foods and even on carb foods already listed, but grown in different countries, and test results continued to accumulate. Consequently, the *International Tables of Glycemic Index* was updated to include glycemic load values in 2002 and published in the *American Journal of Clinical Nutrition*.

That's also when the University of Sydney, Sydney, Australia created a website to host the data so that researchers throughout the world could see what carbohydrate foods had already been tested and thus help identify foods that still needed testing. A certain amount of duplication of tested foods occurred and researchers recognized that *GI* values differed depending on the country, the climate, the soil where the food was grown, and the growing practices used.

In 2008 all acceptable glycemic value test results from 1981 to 2007 were again consolidated into the *International Tables of Glycemic Index and Glycemic Load Values* which was published in the esteemed medical journal *Diabetes Care* in December, 2008. The two tables were published online and made available to scholars and the public as a courtesy by *Diabetes Care,* a prestigious peer reviewed journal published by the *American Diabetes Association*.

That was five years ago from the writing of this book. The newest entry on the *Glycemic Impact timeline* is that Consensus meeting of glycemic experts in June, 2013 in Italy. We have already told you about that meeting in our Introduction. Now that the *Glycemic Load* has finally received the recognition it deserves, in the near future look for another update of *International Tables of Glycemic Index* as new researchers add to and update *Glycemic Load* scores.

APPENDIX D

Warning: These Recipes Are Ultra Low in Carb Content

While the recipes in this book are delicious and easy to prepare, they may be radical for you when it comes to the amount of carbohydrate in each serving. Check with your medical doctor or health care provider for evaluation and any personalized recommendations or restrictions they feel are important for you in your particular case, before you begin any low carb meal plan.

Low Glycemic Happiness has over 120 selections – 30 breakfasts, 30 lunches, 30 dinners, 30 side dishes, and over 30 snacks. You don't have to count calories or study exchange lists to lose weight. Any excess weight you may have will *automagically* begin to disappear almost immediately.

Of course, it's really not magic; it's just the basic science of our physiology. Our recipes are so low in *low glycemic* carb grams that your body simply starts metabolizing any excess fat you may have when you begin eating the meals in the recipes of this book.

We encourage you to eat something every two to three hours. The snacks between meals help provide enduring, slow burning fuel to keep you comfortable and energized throughout your day.

Each of our recipes and snacks list the number of calories and carbohydrates they contain, so you can keep track of them. Glucose is the end product of 90% of all digested carbohydrate. Some people's bodies will use more and others will use less carbohydrate to produce the just right amount of glucose to fuel their active lives.

That's one reason why we urge you to <u>NOT</u> skip any of the three meals and 2 or 3 snacks each day when eating our recipes on a daily, weekly or longer time period. Be sure to eat five or six times a day to provide your body with adequate fuel and nutrients. Most snacks need little or no preparation and may be something as simple as a handful of nuts and a fruit such as a plum or pear. While 5 or 6 meals a day may seem hard to imagine, snacks like a fresh fruit and a handful of nuts are easy to manage.

We urge you to follow these recommendations because the Recommended Daily Allowance (RDA) set for adult individuals is a *minimum of 130 grams of carbohydrate every day.*

This is the current recommendation of the following guiding agencies:

- U.S. Department of Health and Human Service's Office of Disease Prevention and Health Promotion,
- The Centers for Disease Control and Prevention,
- The U.S. Department of Agriculture and
- The U.S. Institutes of Medicine warn that medical research indicates that the human brain needs an Estimated Average Requirement (EAR) of 100 grams of glucose every 24 hours to function efficiently.

The good news is that if you want to eat using recipes from this book every day you can IF you follow this rule: ALWAYS CONSUME AT LEAST 130 grams of carbohydrate. You can easily consume that amount of carbohydrate, even if you are only eating meals from *Low Glycemic Happiness,* if you never skip a meal and always consume not only the main entity for lunches and dinners but also one or two side dishes.

Furthermore, eat often like our grazer ancestors did. Throughout the day, enjoy snacks from our list of recommended snacks. Your brain will get plenty of nourishment. Don't worry about being hungry. While your intake of carbohydrate will be low, if you follow these rules your total amount of calories from food sources other than carbohydrate will energize your body. The result: You will think clearer and be energized throughout the day. Consequently, it will be easier to feel happier.

The End,

But the Beginning of a Healthier Life for You and the Ones You Love

Made in the USA
Middletown, DE
19 November 2021

52901796R00159